DIGGING WITH THE DUCHESS

DIGGING

with the

DUCHESS

Sam Llewellyn

NEW
HAT

Published by
The Marine Quarterly Ltd
The Hope, Lyonshall
Kington
Herefordshire HR5 3HT UK

Telephone +44 (0)1544 340636

Front cover image by Simon Dorrell

ISBN 978-0-9927688-9-8

2

Typeset in Van Dijck at Five Seasons Press
Hereford UK
www.fiveseasonspress.com

Printed by Graficascems, Polígono Industrial
San Miguel 31132 A (Navarra) Spain

CONTENTS

Preface

In 2007 David Wheeler asked if I would write a column about the Hope, where we live, for *Hortus*, Britain's most beautiful gardening journal, of which he is the editor. Something like Schubert's *Winterreise*, but in prose, he said. Well, I am none too keen on Schubert, but I had flu at the time, and was too weak to argue. I therefore wrote a piece based on what I could see from the sickbed, which resembled the *Winterreise* as much as a cabbage resembles a cattleya; then another, then another, until we had about seventy per cent of a decade of the turning year in the garden at the Hope. These columns are the basis of this book.

Over the period of their writing, things have got well out of hand. This is because I know a bit about gardens, but not nearly enough for the hugely erudite *Hortus*. So I was forced to put in bits about the Hope's, er, horticultural *Reise* or trip. And a long, strange trip it's been.

Travelling on your own is all very well, but it is better with companions. I therefore decided that I would make the journey in the company of the Duchess, who is alternately too grand and too drunk to sue. (As you will discover if you read further, she turns out to be a friend in the gelignite category – handy for civil engineering, but capable of frightful destruction.)

Since the day I found her slumped against the Giant's Keyring, the Duchess has infiltrated the garden like bindweed an asparagus bed. Sometimes this causes me to contemplate putting a sign above the gate instructing people to keep out. Sometimes I just write about her tussles with life, gin and fags, in the vague hope that some sort of second-hand confession may cleanse her dark soul. Most of the time, though, I speak as I find. And so, Heaven help us, does she.

Sam Llewellyn
The Hope
2014

A Touch of Flu

IT IS FREEZING OUT THERE. The sun is crawling up through the birch branches. The stair treads are icy under foot. Outside the kitchen window, the shadows of the yews are black lumps on the grass, piped with hoar-frost against the bright green where the sun has already warmed the lawn. Though the sun has not so much risen as heaved itself onto the horizon, and is now rolling along it, too weary to get any higher. I know exactly how it feels.

For what it is worth, this is a Tuesday and it is two months since anyone needed to mow the lawn, and my eyes are definitely not going to open any further because like the rest of me they have got flu and they cannot see the point. There is a fug in the kitchen compounded of coffee and old house and closed windows. Nothing remotely like a thought in the head. Beyond the Jack Frost ferns on the window, the sky is duck-egg blue. Probably the air is exactly like cold vodka. I belt the dressing gown with a length of boat rope and step into steel-toed rigger's boots, ideal slippers because lined with faux fur. I walk out of the door and into the garden.

The air is indeed a bit like cold vodka, but only because cold vodka is quite like cold razor blades, which is what the air is exactly like. From the bottom of the orchard comes the whap of a billhook. My mind instantly slithers back to Norfolk in 1963, coldest winter ever, when we lived in the Rectory between the coast road and the sea. We played ice hockey with walking sticks and a tin lid puck on the lake under the Hall at Glandford. We cooked potatoes in bonfires on the ice, which boomed unnervingly as it grew thicker. One morning the lawn had turned russet. A million or two redwings had flown in from Norway, and were hopping wearily on the frigid grass, too tired to eat. My mother sent me out to the kitchen garden to shoot the pigeons that came volplaning onto the snowbound broccoli, ignoring the sheet-tin Jack Russell terrier cutouts squeaking on their pivots in the hard northeast wind. The gun barrel warmed under my freezing fingers. The pigeons plopped out of the sky and onto the snow, blood-drops like holly berries on their beaks. The marsh was frozen. The beach was frozen. The leaves of the ilexes in the windbreak were the only thing between us and the North Pole. In the far distance, the sea-horizon was a bright steel blue.

Here in my orchard in Herefordshire there was no sea horizon, and I was feeling the lack of it. At the bottom of the orchard, Roger was a small, round figure, scarlet-faced in a cloud of breath-steam. He had taken a chunk out of a thorn trunk and was bending it into the hedge he was pleaching. There were a few red apples on the trees still, and russet thrushes bouncing around after them, not moribund like North Sea redwings, but indecently cheerful, comedy rustics. The stars in their courses are trying to make me cheerful. There is no reason to be cheerful. I want all this red and russet to go away. I want to see something blue.

No such luck. Out of the orchard. Up to the top lawn. Small birds are being relentlessly jolly on the peanuts. The neighbours were shooting yesterday, so the place is overrun with cock pheasants. These are the new pheasants, bred for show and entirely unlike the pheasants of my infancy, naturally selected for a discreet appearance and a retiring demeanour. These ringnecked ponces stem from a gene pool the size of a coffee spoon. They have not even had the brains to get themselves shot. And there they are, swaggering around by the red-gold bark of the *acer griseum*, thinking how festive they look, the morons. They are part of nature's relentless plot to cheer me up. Come on, old chap, a garden is a lovesome thing God wot and if you don't like it you have nobody but yourself to blame because you planted it, look at all those lovely holly berries and Robin Redbreast on the roller and the guelder rose drupes all waxy and luminous, aah.

Turn away. Look for something blue. But the off-white single chrysanthemums are all frosted, and the little pond is frozen grey, and there is nothing to soothe the overheated eye. What I really need is Tresco, with the blue Atlantic heaving at the end of the ilex channels, the Neptune Steps raising a waft of scented geranium at a forget-me-not sky. And instead of these cretinous pheasant-aldermen preening on the lawn, a wisp of woodcock whipping out of the eastern horizon. Not for them a childhood in a pen in the woods, a

few weeks posing on the lawn and a faceful of lead from an insurance
broker. The woodcock are fierce and agile. They have been chased
out of Norway by the frost. When they have restored the tissues in
the mud by the Great Pool they will be off again to Spain, round the
north coast of Africa, up the Tigris, across Georgia and the Black
Sea, and so across the Russian heartlands to Norway again . . .

Blow me down it is cold out here. But the heat in the head rages
unabated. The long-tailed tits are performing circuits and bumps
on the bird table. On a good day they are charming, flying tea-
spoons y'know, but on this particular morning they are the avian
equivalent of spots in front of the eyes. The nuthatch is out, strolling down the post of the bird table to fight it out with the mouse
that has clambered up the post of the bird table. And here comes
the ruddy Greater Spotted Woodpecker. How he keeps his breakfast down God only knows, switchbacking across the sky like that.
Any minute now he is going to be sitting on a hollow tree, jackham-
mering away with his beak. On a morning like this it hurts even to
think about it.

Woe. Woe. My head is hot. I need something blue, and I need it
now.

But the gentians are kipping, and it is a long, long time till litho-
spermums, and the *scilla sibirica* looks as if it has been run over by
a truck. The band of blue between the horizon and the corrugated
asbestos cloud is getting narrower. The house is sprawled yellow
ochre in its winter cheerfulnesses. There are eryngiums and teasels
and superannuated umbelliferae, all filigreed with fussy laces of
frost. In the courtyard of barns the willows blaze merrily, carefully pollarded, red and yellow and deep-red fasciated *sakhalinensis*,
a ruddy bonfire of willow, how can I have planted all this stuff here
and not realised that in the deep midwinter I would need something blue and lovely and wild to cart my poor head away?

Woe. I am shuddering.

The eye skates over the willows. The horse pond is black as jet,
unfrozen, reflecting the frost-pumped crimson of the dogwoods.
More blood to match the lava in my head. Not for long, though.
For the sun is clambering into the cloud layer. Any minute now the
world is going to stop being a ruddy Christmas card and turn into

deep-frozen grey flannel. I am standing in the middle of the yard in my dressing gown and rigger's boots, quite still except for the shuddering, watching the last beam of sun on the last twig of the dogwood before the sun goes out.

There is something blue on the twig. Something remarkably blue, oh yes the blue of an angel's eyes, bluer than gentian or lithospermum or squill or anything else vegetable. Kingfisher blue, in fact.

It is a kingfisher.

The kingfisher dives into the pond and returns to its scarlet dogwood twig. It upends its fish and swallows it. Then it kicks into the air and flips over the barn, heading for the river.

My head is full of kingfisher, large as life and twice as blue.

That's better.

Quite a Lot Happening

THERE HAS BEEN SOME WORK going on in the garden at the Hope. After Christmas the place was a wreck. As always we had shoved a boat into the pond and hauled mistletoe to the masthead. Various junior members of the household snuck into the small collection of crab apple trees (*transitoria*, *spectabilis*) and strung them with fairy lights, the little cautions. Then we trudged round on Twelfth Night and hauled it all down, and waded off through the snowdrops to the South of France, because living in the Welsh Marches in February is like living in a deep-freeze with a mud floor and faulty lights. And when we got back in March, it was time for the wraps to come off.

Literally, in the case of the kitchen garden. All beds had naturally been given a liberal coating of the well-rotted. We had then covered them in sheets of Mypex, a form of plastic permeable to water but not to light, and weighted it down with branches cut off the pollard willows. This looks pretty grim, of course. But once you get your eye in you can persuade yourself that black plastic is merely a form of hardish landscaping, a tidy place on which to gaze among the general shab and frostbite. Meanwhile, under the black surface the worms are busily carting the muck down into the ground. When we took off the plastic the other day, charmingly dark and crumbly vistas were exposed, together with a good stock of mice. These attracted the attention of the local cats and buzzards, and served to remind the philosophical observer that the main business of gardens is sex and death, with beauty a mere by-product.

The wraps are off, the crocuses are going over, and now is the time to enjoy philosophical reflection while you can. The asparagus stands mute under a duvet of couch grass as dense as the reeds in the penultimate sequences of the 'African Queen'. But there is nothing to be done about it, for under the ground the purple-green shoots are heading upwards and will not take kindly to being trampled. So a species of eerie calm pervades the place, carrying the same dramatic weight as the interval between the last tick of the timer and the detonation of the bomb. I am not fooled. In this silence there is work to do. A lot of it. Out in the woods, we do a last-minute swiping-off of hazels level with the ground, trim up pea sticks and reserve, and pile the brash on the stools to thwart the rabbits. Four fat sheaves of wands come back to the barn. That night, the Easter full moon rides up a sky clear enough for frost. But the buds on the briottii horse chestnut are sticky, and there is a mackerel sky, and the glass falls when you tap it. And next morning the world is grey with the kind of fine, warm rain that makes things happen.

My old friend Romke van de Kaa, once head gardener to Christopher Lloyd and nowadays Holland's answer to Roy Lancaster, used to pray aloud for a hormone spray that would cause clipped yews to grow a maximum 2mm a year. Watching the results of the rain throught the breakfast room window, I find myself wishing that there were something similar (organic, naturally) with which we could carpet-bomb the garden at the Hope. But this is ridiculous. All through the winter there has been east in the wind, and we have been wearing jerseys in pairs and socks in foursomes. The equinox has come and gone. The bloody awful Ides of March are behind us, and the sun has leaped on the year's seesaw and brought it crashing down into spring. And any job not yet done can safely be left till next year. We used to live in a giant crumbling ruin in the rainforest of the Blackwater valley in the south of Ireland, where every now and then a surprised gardener would stumble on yet another cottage orné swamped for years under ponticum and oak. If anyone should know how spring can cover up a job undone, we are those people. So come on, Spring, do your worst, I think. We are ready for you. We have the necessary apathy.

The warm days pass. The daffodil buds drop into flowering position and make yellow carpets. Everything starts happening at once.

It is astonishing what will grow in a border when you look away from it for a few days. Blink, and the herbaceous border is a porcupine of shoots, and any day now we will be eating in the open again. And all this time I have been putting off rebuilding the outdoor table. So it is out with the engine hoist and up with the six-by-three flagstone and in with the mixer, and someone is pruning the roses and getting rid of some bindweed and an eryngium that is showing signs of coming back in the wrong place for the fifth year running. The wallflowers are nearly over, and have taken to diffusing a niff that according to an aunt smells exactly like a WAAF barracks hut in 1942. The new table stands by the reflecting pool that brings the light into the kitchen, and I can see that the pool is full of tadpoles, and thrushes with twigs in their beaks are crashing into the quickthorn hedge like gliders landing on Arnhem. The postman is saying good morning, but I cannot hear the exact words over the steady roar of trees pumping water out of the ground and into their brandnew leaves. On the list in my head are items dealing with planting the last of the bare-root trees, too late, too late, and do something about all these dandelions that have appeared on the lawn, and why did you not do all of this earlier in the year instead of sitting in France writing a novel?

Ow.

A flagstone on the foot is not a lovesome thing, God wot. It is however a sign that things have gone far enough. In Villandry they may be hosing down the gravel walks with paraquat, and in the Alcazar at Seville they are deadheading the brugmansias. In the gardens of the Hope, we are washing down arnica pills with whisky as the warm wet night comes down.

Another morning, and the clouds are a grey roof stretching away thirty miles to Clee Hill, and the space under the roof is full to bursting with the song of blackbirds, and the pale green haze round the larches is reminding me why I planted them. In the border a hoe slices through a lily shoot, thank goodness, for that means the end of hoeing and the beginning of hand weeding, which is more fun and can happen during croquet. And best of all here comes Roger, and the mower starts first go, and he is off, a red devil among the banks of rough grass. Nobody takes lawns too seriously round here, except the moles. But as the mower stops, it is good to rest the feet on the new-based stone table, and contemplate the contrast of the smooth newmown with the wild grass around it. It is also good to think that in Scotland the ground is still frozen, and on Tresco the echiums are putting out mighty flower spikes, red and blue, and the garden staff is nervously contemplating the clipping of ilex hedges thirty feet high. But at the Hope, for the first time since last

October we are sitting outdoors drinking tea. And for the first time in weeks, nothing much is happening . . .

Oh yes it is. Any minute now the wild cherries are going to be cathedrals of white foam. Swallows angels ten, and that was definitely a cuckoo.

Here we go.

Summer Sunrise

THE SUN IS RISING, and so am I, and the day looks too good to waste.

In Herefordshire there are at least seventeen words for green, over and above mere shades. There is long grass, mown grass, new yew, cut yew, pondweed and its leprous cousin blanket weed, moss, club-moss, hound's tongue, hart's tongue, polypody and all the other ferns with no name that grow in that wall with no mortar. There is fresh early summer, and leathery late summer. There are envy, nausea, inexperience and hope. And there is the frog motivating across the flagstones towards the pond, and the emerald on the gnarled hand of the Duchess as she digs out a dock in the glaucous shade of the Himalayan whitebeam. Though of course the Duchess will not be up for some time yet.

Oh, yes, this is the forest primeval, hovering on the edge of being completely out of control. I know how it feels.

It is six o'clock, and the birds are still at it like choristers at war. No hum of traffic disturbs the scene. Away they go, echoing down the rides and glades of the Park Wood; of which we are almost a part.

Some people's gardens are like crates full of plants, plonked in landscapes to which they bear no relation. Ardfin, for instance, on the Isle of Jura – a huge stone box, closed now, on a wild, heathery slope heading uphill from the Sea of the Hebrides. Outside, all is heroic and blasted. Inside, *luxe, calme, volupté* prevailed in a delicate jungle of tender plants, and a small marquee of ancient cut dispensed high-grade tea and cake.

Here at the Hope we do not go in for boxes. The idea is for the traveller to be hacking his way through the tangled brakes of the Park Wood, swamped with birdsong and frowning severely at grey squirrels. Gradually, the plant life begins to change. Manna ash replaces ordinary ash. Surely a beneficent nature cannot have planted this grove of 150 walnuts? On the port bow, a dog rose. On the starboard bow, hauling itself through an elder in a spiky mushroom cloud, 'Kiftsgate'. The shoes are soaking wet, and so are the trousers, and the world smells of angelica and woodbine. But suddenly the grass is uncannily short. Dear me, what a lovely morning, ow! (says the notional traveller). This cannot be the forest pri-meval, for I have just tripped over a croquet hoop. Stone me, this is a garden, not a wood.

Where there are croquet hoops there is breakfast. Which on this truly fragrant morning can be taken at the frankly ghastly table beside the frankly beautiful pond. Not so much a pond nowadays, actually, as an aquatic border. Purely by accident, the bankside veg has combined into the happiest of jungles, in which it would be no surprise to collide with a tiger. There is a gunnera (*tinctoria*, not *manicata*, because while I would like this to be Penjerrick or better still Inverewe, it is not) next to a well-shaped dogwood, with a mulberry behind and water soldiers in front. The water is a splendid Rifle Brigade green, and in it there swarm shoals of mutant fish, keen on any spare toast that may be going.

The fish are actually rather important. In the depths of the Park Wood are sludgy hollows where vast tench sieve the ooze for bloodworms. The Hope fish are descended from three goldfish won at Leominster May Fair in 1989, and two golden orfe that arrived from God knows where. The gene pool is therefore tiny, and has produced some very surprising sports. There are triple tailfins, goggle eyes, and red fish piped with black at the margins. The chances of breeding repeat specimens are exiguously small. But as the toast descends, the mind surveys the possibilities. Cuttings? Grown on in the bath? Well, obviously not. What is required is a Korean cloning expert, who will haul forth the germline and grow it on in a chemical soup under ultra-violet light in purpose-built facility in the nettly bit behind the potting shed . . .

There are certainly dangers in early rising followed by too much coffee. It is time for some character-building weeding.

The less said about this the better. Every year brings its own special weed. At first it was docks. Once they were persuaded that it was unfashionable to exist, they were replaced by hogweed, which has been more reluctant to become *vieux chapeau*. When it did finally become so last year, the Lord decreed that cow parsley would enjoy a brief vogue, to be followed by ground elder. This is yielding to digging, but it is a long business and a grim one, and the battle continues until lunch.

This ought really to consist of poached salmon *avec sa mayonnaise et ses nouveaux* spuds *du potager*. Unfortunately the salmon has been replaced by a tin of sardines. But the spuds are indeed here – Arran Pilots, planted on Good Friday as family tradition rightly prescribes, and risen again into a really delicious new potato, as long as you cart them straight from bed to saucepan. Those you are too lazy to dig will grow vast and floury, and make good late-season mashers.

The lunch table is shaded by a specially-maimed lime tree, through whose leaves the sun streams green-gold, splashing the tablecloth beside the luminous projection of the glass of *vin rosé*. A deep hush descends. The birds are presumably having a bit of a siesta, and it seems churlish not to follow their example.

The lime tree is a good place to have a picnic, and to come round an hour after lunch with the marks of grass printed deeply on the face. The evening activity takes place a lot closer to the house. Here, the stone table I installed in the early spring has taken on a monstrous life. The base is a rockery, in which sempervivums and sedums wage war on starvation and drought with the tenacity of their kind. The top is a giant flagstone. The general effect is somewhat tomblike, and lacks only the epitaph. The conversation in the early evening ranges round this. *He Came to Lunch and Now there is Nothing Left?* Possibly. But it was too hot to go carving things, and now it is too late.

Like most outdoor dining rooms in deeper Herefordshire, ours entirely lacks Mexican pot stoves and gas-fired barbecues with integral hostess trolley. It is near the house, which radiates the stored heat of the day. It is alongside a small pond of its own, which provides insects for the bats and a place to cool the wine. It is surrounded by nicotiana and night-scented stocks. And it has a bonfire pit.

This is the thinking person's patio heater, convertible into an incense burner with a branch or two of rosemary from the thickets nearby. The bonfire gets lit, and so do we. The sky deepens and the sun goes down and the colour of the wine changes from pink to deepest red. Man is born to something or other as the sparks fly upward – sorrow? Possibly. Never mind that, let us play just one more tune on the old guitar and look at the hawk-moths ghostly on the honeysuckle, while the rockets of yew and wild cherry carry our space station hurtling through the stars.

But now there is dew on the guitar strings, and the sky is pale, and a blackbird is singing in one of the damson trees. The world is grey, but the sky is going blue, and the greens are going green again, thousands of them, and three hours from now I should be weeding again.

There are however sixty tunes we have not yet played, and enough heat in the fire to make some breakfast. The sun is up again, and so are we, oh dear. Never mind, though. Gather ye rosebuds while ye may. *Chinensis mutabilis*, for preference.

Destiny in Action

T HERE IS A THICKISH, wettish smell in the air, and the lawn has disappeared. The *Acer griseum* and the crab apples are islands in a pearly lake of fog. A matched pair of small, unidentifiable trees is moving across the lake. It is certainly very early in the morning. But no morning is early enough for trees to move. Think hard. The truth dawns at the same speed as the day. These are not trees. They are the antlers of a fallow deer.

Sudden change of mood. The numbness of mind vanishes, swept away by a horrified rush of adrenalin. Below the surface, this fog-lake may be pullulating with roe, sika, muntjac and rabbits. The summer is over, and the autumn is here, and as if the prospect of winter were not grim enough, the lawn is hotching with razor-toothed herbivores bent on demolishing anything with sap in it. It is time to go for the rifle and defend the garden using the only language these furry locusts understand . . .

Calm down. For one thing, I have not got a rifle. For another a big red sun is hauling itself over the horizon, and the mist is blushing faintly as if surprised, and the garden is suddenly looking absolutely beautiful in the usual way, which is to say by accident.

It does not last. The movement of the window catches the deer's eye, and it hops off into the wood, and its slipstream stirs up the fog lake, which coils and winds and dematerialises fast as a ghost. And the sun comes up, and the shadows of the molehills lie across the grey dew, causing another moodswing that can only be the result of low blood sugar. So it is time for a cup of tea, and a soothing contemplation of the prospect framed on its starboard side by a black elder, and on its port side by the cowshed gable with its overgrown John Transom rose, still hanging on to a few ragged red flowers, individually almost odourless but smelling en masse roughly the same as the Earl Grey in the teacup.

The prospect is of Herefordshire, as usual. The outlying fronds of the distant oaks are assuming a faint yellowish tinge. On a morning already made difficult by deer, this is a further incitement to moodswing. A month fron now the great oaks of the Arrow Valley will be leafless black dishmops, the hedges grim black entanglements. There will be no colour anywhere, and night will fall like a wet sack at three p.m.

Enough. The sun is up now, It is time for a tonic blast of the herbaceous border. Many of my sophisticated gardening friends have rules about such borders. Yellow flowers have no place in them, they say, and the same goes for dahlias. Naturally I respect their opinions, honed to a shaving edge of perfect taste by decades of stropping on white gardens and species rhododendrons. But I also respect the opinion of my friend and neighbour George the Postman, a splendid horticulturalist and an authority on the flora and culture of the Mynydd Eppynt, the hills that hunch their heathery shoulders behind Llandrindod Wells. The garden of George's garden is an inferno of dahlias. Last spring he pressed on us a couple of boxes of tubers the size of King Edwards. Now they are sulphur-yellow triffids six feet high, interspersed with Bishop of Llandaff and *Rosa chinensis mutabilis*, and some tasty red sedums closer to ground level. The general effect is that Bonfire Night has arrived a month early, and jolly nice too, because no dark thought can survive this much red and yellow.

The frost will knacker them, of course. I will leave the tubers to take their chances in the ground, and the border will go into late autumn mode, featuring chrysanthemums. Unlike the dahlias, these are a model of discreet good taste. There has been no disbudding, no paper bags, and there are no pompoms, cabbages, or nuclear explosions the size of babies' heads. These chrysanthemums are single and whitish, tinged with a little blue here, a little pink there. Nobody knows what they are called, because I got them from my mother, and she got them from hers, who probably got them from hers in about 1890. They vouchsafe their hushed elegance in November, and the merest whisper of Gardeners' Question Time causes their petals to slam tight shut.

The dew is still on the yew blocks, each globular drip holding a vision of a tiny garden in its crystal ball. I can tell without consulting these that what the future holds in this particular corner is not much, as the squirrels have nicked the cob nuts and the walnuts. In the kitchen garden, however, we have been taking a leaf out of their book, and preparing for winter.

The asparagus topknots are peroxide yellow, awaiting the chop. The spinach beet is the colour and texture of old mackintosh. The leeks are waiting to do their Welsh stuff in the dank months ahead. There are parsnips. Other than that there is a lot of bare earth awaiting muck and Mypex, because what was on it or in it is now safely in sacks and jars and big boxes of dry sand. The tomatoes were a failure this year. Not so the chillies. For reasons unfathomable, bushes calculated to bear a couple of ounces of red-hots bore a couple of pounds instead. There are round ones and thubby ones and snaky conical objects, ranging in colour from slime green to fire-engine red. What they have in common is a violent, searing, blacksmith's-forge-in-the-tropics, metal-runs-like-water heat. Eating them is like sending your tongue for a holiday on the planet Mercury. And there are about forty pounds of them. It looks as if a few stone will have to go to the Harvest Festival. Having been displayed, the produce is donated to the Griffin Home for the Aged. They have no idea what is about to hit them.

We have started lighting fires in the afternoon. The apple trees that blew over last year have dried nicely, and are dispensing a pleasing reek from the grate. The Duchess is drinking lapsang souchong out of a bone china cup, her engagement sapphire (lost twice this week and dowsed for successfully both times) contrasting agreeably with her filthy fingernails. And the sky is still clear, and the light is bouncing off the reflecting pool outside the kitchen window and bursting in golden ripples on the ceiling.

We have finally thought of something to do with the Canadians who are staying. They have come back from Hergest Croft, where the maples are blazing merrily. Now they are clucking over the sugar maple that is dying by inches in a corner of the lawn, and the sumac thicket known to its enemies as VFS, or Visible from Space. And ignoring the true preparations for winter being made by the mahonias, shuttlecocking away fit to bust, and the *viburnum bodnantense* getting ready for action behind a discreet screen of leaves.

It has turned out well, this day – not only misty, but mellow and on the whole fruitful. Soon it will be time for the goose quill and the squid ink, and perhaps a strengthening glass of St-Joseph. But first, a last gloating stroll round the kitchen garden in order to get the full blast of contrast between the warm life indoors and the owl-haunted dark outside. And there it lies in the last of the light, all ready to be tucked up for the winter –

Wait a minute. Wait a *minute*.

The heartbeat accelerates. There in the brassica cage are two great big half tame bigeared ringnecked fatarsed thickheaded cock pheasants. They have eaten half the cabbages and they are starting on the other half. Curse their nasty stupid greenshadowed eyes, how are we supposed to fight off scurvy in the deeps of winter when these blasted lawn ornaments are ripping up our main source of Vitamin C? And all for the passing gratification of heavily armed bank directors bluing their absolutely underserved bonuses on heedless slaughter? To hell with mellow fruitfulness. I want a gun, and I want one now. In the garden survival is the watchword, and it is won at gunpoint, and its accompaniments are game chips and gravy. Made with crab apple jelly. A dozen jars of which went into the cupboard last week –

In autumn, you can practically hear the wheels of Destiny going round.

What Shall We Do with the Snowbound Aesthete?

O N THE FACE OF IT, this is not a great moment for aesthetes in the garden. The weather is vile. Things that are actually growing, like leeks, may be greenery-yallery but are certainly not Grosvenor Gallery. The borders are shabby wrecks, deliberately left untidy to give shelter to ladybirds and queen wasps and possibly, given where we live, a few SAS men. And the tasks that remain before closedown are muddy and brutal. Take, for instance, the annual pogrom against *Senecio tangutica*, which has spent a cheerful summer trying to throttle the golden bamboo, and must now be taught a sharp lesson.

Tangutica's nine-foot spikes of yellow flowers are matched underground by tubers whose lower surfaces bristle with leg-like roots. Presumably it is these legs that the plant uses to run, which it does at high speed and in all directions. If the legs don't catch you the seeds sure will, for the excavation of the tubers takes place in a cloud of down similar to that of *tangutica*'s cousin the groundsel, and easily as fertile.

Well, the excavations eventually ceased, and a few hundred early red tulips went in to brighten up the bamboo stems. Then the rain came down with associated sleet and frosts. And the garden vanished under a sheet of mud, becoming something glimpsed occasionally through a steamed-up window, lowering shabbily at an equally shabby sky. The aesthete pines for frost sparkling on the spidery skeleton of an agapanthus flower. What the aesthete actually gets is rain sliming a frost-rotten agapanthus leaf. This is a signal provided by nature to tell you it is time to fall back on your inner resources.

Inner resources are unevenly distributed. Some people have none, and must beguile the long dark afternoons by throwing playing cards into a top hat. Others have far too many, and will not shut up about them. The Duchess lies somewhere between the two extremes, though it is hard to tell exactly where, for she has locked herself in the library, where she is chain-smoking Capstan

Full Strength and drinking Navy rum, her sapphires catching the reading light as she leafs through Sutton's catalogues of the 1950s. At these times, as at most others, it is best to pay her no attention other than keeping the doors shut and the windows open. Anyway, there are the visiting flower arrangers to contend with.

These turn up pretty continuously. The kitchen is full of whacking great jars of *Lonicera purpusii*, which smells lemonily delicious until the door closes behind the arranger. At this point all the flowers fall on the table and it is time to shuffle into the fog and cut some more. (Fortunately, *purpusii* is an explosive bush of Napoleonic ambitions, so it doesn't hurt.) Persistent arrangers are directed to the *Viburnum bodnantense*, now blazing away on its bare stalks and emitting powerful whiffs of hair-oil, and the astonishing *Clematis armandii*.

Armandii has been a bit of a revelation. In my childhood, I loathed it. The clatter of its dark, fish-shaped leaves in a February breeze opens the shutters on Proustian vistas of numb feet and mittened fingers freezing to shotgun barrels. And its spidery white flowers are all very remarkable so early, or possibly late, but then so is a two-headed cat, and how many of those do you want hanging around the house? So until recently I turned up my nose at this clematis, and so now does the flower arranger, turning her attention to the *Mahonia japonica*, whose eye-watering fumes of lily-of-the-valley bring to the Hope's medieval vaulting a whiff of the Streatham Locarno in 1963.

Recently, though, I discovered that I was wrong about *armandii*. So today out I nip, and cut some good strands, and stick them in a vase by the fire. And when they warm up, the flower arranger's neck jolts round with an audible click, and her nose whiffles. Because *armandii* smells *terrific*.

In the gamut of smells, pundits have identified 1) polite and cheerful (roses, pinks, and come to that *Lonicera purpusii*) and 2) rude and brooding (jasmine, stephanotis). *Clematis armandii* fits firmly and powerfully into Category Two. For a plant that is the opposite of tropical, this seems weird. Perhaps it is making a special effort to attract the attention of any frostproof bees that may be mucking about in early Feb. Whether or not this is true, it comes on like Lord Byron – lewd, seductive, and perpetually scheming to clamber up the drainpipe and into the wife's bedroom while no one is looking.

Cut flowers, no matter how niffy, will beguile a winter, but they will not get you through it. The true aesthetic journey is littered with man-made objects. This means sculpture. At its most basic level, this can involve a *Three Graces* moulded in cement at one half scale, the Graces apparently conducting a bad-tempered argument about who did what to whom in the episode of *East Enders* they glimpsed from the lawn last night. At the other extreme are the conceptual structures of CDs and string that protect cabbages from pigeons. These look nearly as bad as the Graces. Furthermore they do not stop pigeons, on whom symbolism is wasted, and who understand only the language of hot lead. (Recent research in Africa, however, claims that CD installations do deter elephants from visiting gardens. Apparently the pachyderms are clever enough to interpret the reflections from the CDs as the flashing torches of people who may also be carrying gigantic rifles.) The conclusion is this: in non-African regions, the only things that garden sculpture should be expected to stop are boredom and vistas.

The basic Hope sculpture is a found object, that is, an abandoned garden roller, *circa* 1860, too heavy to pull any further and left to fester. More formally, the boys once welded up a montage of old Ford parts and a bow tie, which was called Your Escort for the Evening until someone drove into it. More wholemeal and in keeping are the large wooden sculptures known as Giants' Keyrings. These take as their inspiration the tenon ends of the tie-beams of roof-trusses. Observers with exceptionally powerful imaginations can come to see them as representations of eight-foot monks standing in contemplation, shoulders hunched, hands thrust deep into the pockets of their habits. They have a pretty rough finish, partly to attract lichen and partly because they were made with chainsaws in a hurry. But they provide perches for flycatchers in summer and mole-spotting cats in winter. And they stop a vista dead in its tracks.

Not that they are a patch on Michael Black's garden in north Oxford. Black is the sculptor who recarved the neo-Classical heads on the Sheldonian Theatre when the limestone originals melted in the Thames Valley's acid rain. The acute observer may notice a certain toothlessness among the emperors, or philosophers, or whatever they are. This is because Black was in the habit, while carving the heads, of presenting lady visitors to his studio with stone teeth knocked out of the Ancients' gobs. In his garden, massive box topiary piles skyward, flanked by soaring birds that on closer inspection prove to be carved out of farm shovels with an angle grinder. A vast woman, apparently moulded from life, rides a gigantic bicycle. And a colossal structure of crumpled aluminium foil reclines outside the kitchen window; though a critical scrutiny reveals that it is not aluminium foil, but chromed sheet steel, crumpled by God knows what Titanic forces.

Ah, well. Lunch is over, and the night is creeping in, and black clouds with yellow bellies are lumbering out of the north. Soon it will snow, and we can forget about plants and start tracking animals across the surface. We can also forget about sculpture. At times like these, aesthetes get out there and build snowmen.

The Spring Express

WINTER WENT ON a bit too long. Well after it should have ended there we still were, slumped on the sofa, gazing slack-jawed at twenty-six condemned cock pheasants eating a hearty breakfast in the herbaceous border. The ground appeared to be made of tarmac dusted with sea salt. The Gatling seemed jammed, the Colonel dead. Then one morning I woke laughing hysterically from a dream in which I had just made tea for the bank manager by infusing the compost heap in a bucket, and felt a sort of juddering in the cosmos, as if a mighty steam train was thundering towards us over a bumpy track. And there suddenly was the Spring Express, panting and roaring and spewing energy in all directions.

When this particular train pulls into the station there is no time for hanging around, because it is not going to wait, and the station-master is drunk and the porters are asleep, so there is no help to be had. All you can do is hurl your bags into the goods van and jump after them, and stagger like James Bond over the wagon roofs to the footplate to see if you can drive this thing before it drives you.

First there was a hasty but satisfying phase of bonfiring up the debris of hedge-laying and the brashings of the walnut grove before some thick but delightful bird could decide that this pile of dead stuff was a handy nesting site. Then there were the ponds to weed.

Actually there are three ponds. The rectangular tank positioned to reflect light into the kitchen is a tidy, polite object, containing two fish and a pink water-lily. It can safely be ignored. So, for a different reason, can the tangled morass of bullrush and Norfolk reed we planted to attract warblers. The warblers have ignored it in a studied manner, and its vegetation is now totally beyond control. Its only use is as an object of idle speculation. The leaves of the Norfolk reed, for instance, are of a supremely attractive stripiness, and would make a pleasing if ephemeral material for a gent's suiting. They are also handy for sucking up foul water and wafting heavy metals into the breeze, assuming they can find any heavy metals lying around in their bucolic corner.

The pond that needs the attention is bigger and better than either of these, and sits pretty much at the heart of things, crowned, in summer, with a whirling column of swallows and martins eating the bugs it produces. It is a relic of a time when the Hope was a hive of eighteenth-century agro-industry. Much work took place in the sheds around the yard. The sheds are linked by a sort of cobbled quay that makes a walkway a couple of feet above the level of the yard, which in bygone winters was rendered swampy by the presence of a herd of gigantic Hereford cattle, mooing and chewing hay. The swampiest corner of all never really dried out. So when we came to gardenise the yard, I had a quick dig there with a spade, and the hole filled up with water. Then we summoned Tony Griffiths, who is rumoured to weed his carrots with the bucket of his JCB, and Tony removed three hundred and fifty tons of red sludge from the wet corner, creating an elegantly-contoured hole eight feet deep which instantly filled with water and has remained full ever since through summers dry and wet. It now bears a fine crop of water-lilies, water soldiers and kingcups, and is lined with dogwoods, flag irises and a gunnera. There is also a mulberry tree that is supposed to drop its berries into the mouths of waiting golden carp, but doesn't. As well as this charming and intentional vegetation, there are weeds.

These started with a few strands of Canadian pondweed, which have multiplied astonishingly. Then there is some stuff that the local bat expert identified as New Zealand stonecrop, which may have arrived on a heron's foot, and duckweed, which may have arrived on the heron's other foot. The positive here is that between them these horrors pour in so much oxygen that blanket weed – the worst horror of all – hyperventilates and can gain no toehold, while the fish, newts, dragonflies, frogs, toads, and presumably brontosauri where available, thrive astonishingly. The negative is that if left unchecked, they would remove any trace of open water, making the pond hideous and impossible to navigate, which would be a grave disappointment to tiny Vasco da Gamas come summer.

The equipment for weeding is simple. You need a rake, and a wetsuit, and a pair of chest waders left over from the salmon fishing, and a prospective daughter-in-law. All of the above plunge in, me in the waders, daughter-in-law in the wetsuit. My job is to give instructions, identify tricky plants and succour challenged newts and dragonfly larvae. The daughter-in-law's role is to take great gasping breaths, rake Canadian pond-weed out by the roots, and attach a surplus boat anchor to the rhizomes of the water-lilies so that her future husband can heave them up the bank with a tractor. These water-lily rhizomes are roughly the size and shape of the saltwater crocodiles of northern Australia. Like the crocodiles, they are said to be slightly edible, though unlike the crocodiles, they do not eat you back.

Eventually, the veg gets detached from the bottom of the pond and left in piles by the margins to facilitate newt exit. Then we go and have tea and talk loudly to blot out the roar of rising sap. It is at this point that someone usually suggests tapping the birch trees in order to make wine. The standard reply is that there is plenty of good wine coming out of France these days, and there is no sense going round boring birches half to death to harvest a low-level emetic.

The Scandalous Border is coming up nicely. This is a shady spot in which we bury bulbs when they have finished flowering indoors. Quite a lot of hyacinths and narcissi actually survive, and the effect, against a sombre background of long-over *Mahonia japonica* and evergreen ferns, is pretty startling. But cheerful, cheerful.

Equally startling are the Yew Teeth. This is a row of eight yews cut into square-sided lumps, rising from gums of polyanthus calculated to dazzle the postman. They are best left to fend for themselves until the new bronze yew shoots turn green and leathery. More difficult this year are several cistuses dripping over a drystone wall in which we have planted an alpinetum of succulent saxifrages and sedums and sempervivums. Cistuses are very good fun for about a week in high summer. Otherwise they sit looking grey-green as the Limpopo, obviously wishing they were back home on a Mediterranean hillside taking their chances with the local goats. But nobody here has the moral courage to heave them out and start again.

The solution we are planning this year is to put climbers through them. Honeysuckle is no good, as we have discovered by combining it with a yucca, with whose help it has become a totally unapproachable hybrid of hedgehog and octopus. *Tropaeolum speciosum*, favourite of all favourites for its splendid red, seems to enjoy itself some years, but not most others; besides which it likes cold and wet, whereas cistus likes hot and dry. There is a good crawling monkshood that we once found in Liz Taylor's Whimble Nursery, though its blue is somewhat funereal. Best of all, though, there is outside the back door a big purplish sage bush with an ordinary blue *Clematis macropetala* scrambling through it. This works like a charm. Furthermore, wild clematis grows alongside wild cistus in the mountains of Mallorca, and for all I know elsewhere. So clematis it will be for the cistus. And if we sow quite a lot of stocks in the gaps, it will not matter that we have breached the Smelly Flowers Only policy in this part of the garden . . .

Look out. Planning is one thing. Getting swallowed up by dreams of summer is another. It will probably rain all year for the third year running. Well, if it does we are ready for it. We have planted plenty of *Salix viminalis* in a boggy patch in the new wood, coincidentally located quite close to the septic tank soakaway. The pruning has been going on for a while now, inspired by Jenny Crisp, willow grower and maker of Britain's most beautiful baskets. Jenny has woven willow into the frankly uninspiring iron railings of her Victorian school near Eye church, Herefordshire's finest; and now they are beautiful objects, full of rhythm and grace. It is my plan to do roughly the same thing at the Hope, but more crudely, obviously. The Duchess is squelching around the *viminalis* now. By the grim grey look of her I suspect she is planning a wicker coffin. Best look at something else, really.

And there is plenty to look at. A soft thick rain is falling, and plants are roaring volcanically out of the ground, and the red tulips are gorgeous beside the golden bamboo, as planned. The Spring Express is thundering on towards summer, and there are no brakes, and the regulator is lashed wide open, and there is actually no need for anyone on the footplate. It is a warm sort of rain. Ideal for drinking a greenish wine in, really. Buffet car ho!

A Voyage in the West

THE SOLSTICE HAS COME AND GONE. The sundial's shadow is a little black pool in the moss under the gnomon. It is hot and green – sweltering hot, and so green that the mind wanders nostalgically back to Hergest and a red *Rhododendron* 'Elizabeth' in front of a cool white-barked *Betula jacqmontii* 'Jermyns', with behind it the clear pink of a big *Magnolia campbelli* . . .

Someone is sneezing on the far side of the hedge. They are high, cross sneezes, so the sneezer is the Duchess. Her blood is deepest azure, splendidly reactive, so she is allergic to just about everything. The situation is aggravated by the fact that she has declared a state of economic siege, dismissed all garden help, and taken on her own bony shoulders the Hope's grimmer chores. The dawn chorus segues seamlessly into the howl of her chainsaw. After a light breakfast of anchovies and gin, she careers wildly to and fro on the lawnmower, cursing all trees. This process naturally stirs her allergies to fever pitch, forcing her to spend the afternoon on a daybed in the Turkish kiosk, smashed comatose on Piriton and smoking Capstan Full Strength against the wasps. At dusk she zigzags forth to reminisce.

The other night she gazed upon our flaming embothrium, flared her nostrils to a whiff of wood smoke, and started talking about Lochinch Castle. A friend of hers visited this pile in the time of the last Lord Stair but two, famous as a man who would shoot his own grandmother if he saw her rising from a root field. Returning to the castle one afternoon, the friend became aware of a delicious, incense-like smell. He asked what it was. 'Embothrium,' said Stair, waving at the castle's forest of chimneys. 'Never burn anything else.' This seemed to impress even the Duchess. Your embothrium is generally considered a shrubby object of no great height or bulk, and the fireplaces of Lochinch were apparently on a scale that required the service of a full-time stoker. The Gulf Stream coast of Scotland is evidently pretty useful embothrium country. So why were we hanging around in the Welsh Marches?

During the week that followed, we painted the boat. Then we hauled up some sails and went to sea, heading west into a more or less sneeze-free zone.

Many of the great gardens of the British Gulf Stream were made before roads and even railways, and are designed to be approached and supplied by sea. There exists a splendidly vituperative mid nineteenth-century correspondence between the strong-minded Augustus Smith, founder of Tresco, and the equally firm-willed Hooker of Kew. The difficulty was Smith's hijacking of a consignment of mesembryanthemums from a Kew-bound ship. Their bellowings, expressed in the blackest of ink on foolscap folded quarto, produced a *froideur* that lasted some ten years.

The Foxes of Falmouth were more pacific, as befitted a gardening family with its roots sunk deep in Quakerdom. Astonished visitors to the garden of Robert Were Fox at Rosehill found themselves picking lemons from trees in the open ground. His descendants, seeking to spare their families the diseases brought to Falmouth by ships from all over the world, moved out of town to found the valley gardens of Trebah, Glendurgan and Penjerrick. We sailed from Falmouth on a hot morning, and thumped for a couple of hours across a sea that walloped brine into our eyeballs. At last the shores of the Helford River drew together ahead, and the anchor rattled down under the dour grey buildings of Glendurgan village.

Ashore it was all sea-bleach and orange lichen. But as we walked into the valleys, the air stilled and the world changed, becoming muffled and green. Trebah, westernmost of the Fox valley gardens, depends on the tourist trade for its prosperity. Its trees are splendid, and its paths wind charmingly around the stream. A Zen monk might find the gee-whizz factor a bit high, but children love it, for they can swing like apes from the ropes provided and act the maggot to their hearts' content. Monks will be fine at Glendurgan, and so will older people; for it is run by the National Trust, and is as a result hushed, reverent and accessible to all. Foxes still inhabit the house, comfortable and ungrand at the head of the valley. From the terrace it is a joy to contemplate the maze writhing intestinally up the western slopes, and admire the placing of the trees, which show to brilliant advantage from the lawn. Charles, the Fox in possession and author of a useful book on Glendurgan, claims that during the planting of the trees, his ancestor patrolled the terrace with a megaphone, directing the operations of vast squads of labourers moving reeling towers of scaffolding simulating copper beeches and magnolias. After all, there is probably nothing worse than finding you have planted a hundred-foot copper beech eighteen inches too far to the east.

But when the Cornish sun blazes out of a sky of brass, or the Cornish drizzle weeps out of a sky of wet felt, Penjerrick is the place to be. It may be a bit disorderly for monks, and a bit slippery for valetudinarians. The anchorage is dodgy in some breezes, and it is a slight hike from the beach. But once you are in, the trees meet overhead, and a whiff of fox tangles in the ferns as you shoulder your way down the narrow paths. Where the stream has made the ground swampy underfoot, there is a proper gunnera jungle. This is not the polite, rather *voulu* gunnera thicket of other Cornish gardens, charming in its way, but carefully sculpted by strong men with sharp spades. This is the honest-to-goodness forest primeval, in whose pathless wastes the intrepid traveller can sit undisturbed on a stump and while away the afternoon looking up at the shadowplay of insects wandering to and fro across leaves backlit lime-green between the cathedral tracery of the ribs.

A long day's sail further west, St Michael's Mount was doing its stuff. We went alongside in the harbour, crashed across an enormous meadow of red-hot pokers and started scaling the cliff-faces towards the lair of the giant disposed of by Jack. This is a garden comprehensively replanted between 1976 and 2004 by my redoubtable aunt Helen Dorrien Smith, herself a daughter of Tresco Abbey. The rockery and the final approach to the Mount's Victorian wing are now pretty much Tresco in style. The lower lawns, narrow and merely sloping, gaze out at a vast expanse of sea and sky over margins planted with (among other things) scented geraniums, purewhite deeply unhardy dimorphothecas, and black aeoniums. The rock steepens as it rises, the terraces hacked out of the living rock now, walled on their seaward sides with an eighteenth-century cunning that directs the wind straight upwards; so that on a day when the breeze has scoured away every atom of haze, you can stand on the terrace and watch gulls fighting for a grip on the racing air, while behind you the leaves of the *Sparmannia africana* on the wall are moved to no more than a slight, non-committal rustle.

Out there on the horizon, Scilly is a series of blue crayon-lines hull-down in bright Atlantic.

'Tresco?' said the Duchess.

Tresco is a hard place to sail to, because the wind is always in the wrong direction. Besides, the cabin was filling up with plastic bags of cuttings. And the sun had been shining for so long that the weather had really got to break, and the trees would thrash around like inside-out umbrellas, and this extremely small boat would start behaving as if it was stuck in a washing machine.

'Home,' I said.

So it was away across Mount's Bay, and round Land's End into the Bristol Channel. By the time we got into the Severn we had had about enough of salt wind and razor-sharp light. We were ready for some green in the air, and less of the fiery rum, and more of the golden light percolating through the lime tree and the glass of Château de Sours deep, bright pink on the table under it.

And here we are. The smelly geraniums have rooted, and the *Luma apiculata* probably never will, but we are not amazed, by this or anything else. For the tower of swallows is back over the pond, and the click of ball on ball means that lawn sports, slow but ferocious, are on the go. And someone has lit the barbecue, and someone else is tuning a guitar by the bonfire. The smoke smells good tonight. Not of embothrium, for the Hope specimen is a mere bush. We are burning *leylandii* scavenged from someone's mangled hedge. It makes fine aromatic firewood, showing that however grim a thing may seem it is probably useful for something. And here come the stars. The weather in the far south-west has gone bloody awful, but we don't care. Out with the corks, and onward to moonrise!

North and South

THAT SMELL IS IN THE AIR AGAIN. It is thick and wet, with a faint hint of mould. The dew is not so much a dampness as an inundation, and the pheasants leave dark trails as they wade through the grass. In the outer reaches of the garden, where it merges into the woods, the deer prowl and prowl around, ready to pounce on the half-ripe leaders of the five-year trees. Autumn is coming, and as usual we are in a hurry.

This was not always the case. A month ago we were in Loch Hourn, a fjord that runs some fifteen miles eastward out of the Sound of Sleat, the body of water that separates southern Skye from the Scottish mainland. Hourn means 'Hell', and the mountains leap from the black waters of the loch in a series of thousand-foot cliffs that would have had Dante scribbling notes on the back of an envelope. It was into this loch in the late nineteenth century that Bob Birkbeck sailed his steam yacht. He liked what he saw, so he bought thirteen thousand acres of the north shore, and in a favoured spot established a large and comfortable lodge. Unlike most post-Balmoral settlers, he did not limit himself to shooting the local deer. He observed that parts of his new estate were somewhat protected from frost, so he fenced off fifty acres and established what was then the biggest eucalyptus plantation in the northern hemisphere, interplanted with the usual rhododendrons and laced with vertiginous paths hacked out of the living rock.

During the hundred-odd years that followed, the rhododendrons' *ponticum* rootstocks turned the whole place into an impassable jungle. A recent programme of managed destruction by dauntless volunteers has finally excavated a seaside garden on a gigantic scale, through which burns crash hundreds of feet down polished falls and chutes veined with quartz. There are eucryphias, crinondendrons, enkianthus. There is a singularly fine *Sequoia sempervirens*, and arguably the most beautiful *Hoheria lyallii* in the world, cool grey and bridal-white against its backdrop of crag and foreshore. This must be one of the wildest gardens in Britain, made wilder by the gum trees' new habit of dropping gigantic branches without warning,

and the fact that it is invisible for much of the year because wrapped
in dirty scarves of cloud.

At the seaward end of the loch is Li, built by Rick and Hillary
Rohde. Li sits on the north shore of the Knoydart peninsula, three
miles by sea from the nearest road. Thirty years ago, the Rohdes
fenced off a hundred acres of bare mountain. Within five years the
enclosure was covered with naturally regenerated birch and Scots
pine, which now shelter a charming garden of rhododendrons, the
low-lying areas being populated with outrageously healthy roger-
sias and gunneras and other bog enthusiasts, just touched when
we visited by the first cool breath of the early northern autumn.
Instead of statuary at the end of its rides, Li has mighty mountains.
Where other gardens have fishponds, Li has the blue Atlantic. We
watched our boat rocking gently at anchor beyond the garden shed.
Suddenly it was surrounded with huge black sickle fins: a dozen
pilot whales, appearing from behind a rhododendron bush and exit-
ing stage left. The Duchess lit a meditative Capstan Full Strength.
I could read her thoughts like the neon in Times Square. Koi carp?
she was thinking. You can keep 'em.

Feeling deeply inadequate, we took ship for the warmer South.

In the Welsh Marches it was still late summer, murmurous with
bees from the hives in the orchard and full of the gamey niff of
the last flush of roses. In the weeks that followed we embarked on
the usual frenzy of pickling and jamming and this and that, while
the Duchess wafted around looking severe and decapitating Baby
Bear pumpkins with Jacobin zeal. It has been a good damson year,
so naturally she took charge of manufacturing the gin. Now she is
slumped in a corner of the library, emitting fumes and watching
the distant hills. 'It is coming,' she murmurs from time to time. 'It
is coming.'

And of course she is right. The year is on the move, and so are
we. Above twelve hundred feet, far above the picking and press-
ing and eye-watering boiling in vinegar, where the cottages crouch
behind the pine belts that stop the potatoes blowing out of the
ground, a leaf is turning. And down the hill sweeps autumn, gath-
ering momentum. The maples and dogwoods catch fire. The larches
once again demonstrate that they are better value than most official
garden trees, turning a rusty brown that looks like the taste of

medlars. (The next best thing to the deciduousness of a larch is the deciduousness of a *Metasequoia glyptostroboides*. As a family we have a soft spot for this living fossil. It was discovered in China in 1941. One of the first specimens planted in captivity is in the garden of the British Embassy in Kathmandu. Long acquaintance with the specimen in the garden at the Hope led our son Will to recognise it after he had emerged reeking from the Nepalese wilds, the recognition earning him the goodwill of the wife of the Ambassador. This kind woman lushed him up with tea and biscuits as a result, and even arranged for his foul clothes to be washed. It is impossible not to respect a genus of tree that is not only among the most ancient known, but also gets the family laundry done at government expense.)

Autumn is a good season for memory. The poet Schiller was famously unable to compose unless he could smell rotting apples. I know how he felt. In the autumn reorganisation, just about everything reminds me of something else. The orchard takes care of the rotting apple department. The hebe cuttings we are potting on, swiped with permission from a particularly brilliant seedling near Dunkerton's Cider Mill in this corner of Herefordshire, bring back the taste of Dunkerton's light, bright perry. The Virginia creeper rambling blood-red across the workshop reminds me that I have been meaning to dig the ruddy thing up for years. And the silky autumn pompoms of the *Clematis orientalis* on the gable are smelling of hot metal in a way that brings to mind the ancestral tinplate works in South Wales.

The year is moving on. The Wye and Lugg are in spate, and rocks are rolling in the riverbed of the soul. The sky gets lower, and the days get shorter, and the deer are out in the open now, pruning away in broad daylight, curse them, so we will end up not with the new wood we planned, but with five acres of *ad hoc* topiary. But there is no time to worry about this, because the equinoctial gales brought down a sixty-foot wild cherry, and the straight bit needs to go off for planks, and the rest needs to be cut up into preternaturally elegant firewood. And there is a fifteen-foot stump remaining. The summer was not all that great, as the Duchess never tires of explaining to anyone who will listen. Polyannas among her acquaintance, including me, reply that this merely increases the odds that next year will be better. And it is this thought that suggests that the bust stump of the cherry will make a fine base for a gazebo or drinking platform, of the kind built at Highgrove on the stump of a deceased cedar, or in the branches of an ash tree by the great Herefordshire designer Nick de St Croix. So what with putting things to bed for the winter and starting to build for next year, there is pretty much a frenzy going on: which is also true of the squirrels, and the jays, and presumably the plants, hauling the sugars down into their roots and getting ready for a really constructive dormancy during which they will get a lot of things done.

The mountains around Loch Hourn have already passed from autumn yellow to winter white. There will be one final day of the great trees of the Marches, natives and Himalayan immigrants, standing rust-coloured against a bright blue sky. Then the weather will come spinning out of the Atlantic, and the late chrysanthemums will bow down, and the sedums will thank their lucky stars that they are low, ground-hugging creatures. The sun will set low and pale and ominous, and by its light we will examine a last blast of fuchsia through the deeps of the gin. And that night the rain will roar on the panes, and the apple-smoke whoof down the chimney. And next morning the lawns will be yellow and red, and the trees will be nude, and it will be winter.

Time for Another Bonfire

So here we are again. The nights are like wet black curtains, parting briefly to let some grey daylight seep in. There is moaning in the kitchen garden, moaning in the borders, moaning at the bar. It is time to sort the apples, separating the sheep from the goats, for there are far too many of them; then beat a retreat to the studio. It is warmish in the studio, and in front of the big window a profusion of cuttings is clinging grimly to life.

There is no heated glass at the Hope, and the cold frames are very cold indeed, and propagation gets done not when it ought to be done but when someone gets round to it. So these cuttings were mostly taken in late summer, and desire to be launched into the world for hardening-off any time now. The way the world is at the moment, though, they will be less hardened off than frozen solid, like the *Acer griseum* seeds sulking in the bed the far side of the window. So there they sit, squadrons of whitefly droning through their upper fronds, waiting without much hope for spring.

Among the cuttings are outcrops of pelargonium, to remind me of Cornwall and bring a faint breath of the sub-tropics to the chilly Marches. None of your 'Lady Plymouth' here, infinitely less beautiful than its human namesake and with a thin niff of toothpaste. These are the deep-red rose-scented festoons that avalanche down the Neptune Steps at Tresco, whose warm winters keep them growing from year to year under the Atlantic sky. A sky which at this time of year sometimes cruises north as far as Herefordshire; at which point it is an idea to abandon the verminous *hortus siccus* developing under the studio window, and head for the outdoors.

The winter patrol is a somewhat straitened affair. It is always good to check the gunnera, sprawled on the side of the pond with its leaves folded over its crown like the beast from the *Mappa Mundi* that sleeps wrapped in its gigantic ears. The dogwood is admiring its gory reflection in the big pond. The Duchess is flitting among the long shadows of the molehills, counting the number of flowers out. She cannot rid herself of this habit, acquired when she lived with her wicked mother just inland from Monte Carlo. But continuing it is a disaster for the gin, as it does not cheer her up at all. Quite the opposite, for the midwinter list is depressingly short. There is the carpet of polyanthus from which the dark fangs of yew rise beside the yard. There is the *Viburnum bodnantense*, the *Lonicera purpusii*, the winter jasmine and the *Clematis armandii*. There are some croci and snowdrops and Siberian squills and self-sown grape hyacinths, which she thinks look so constipated that she scarcely classifies them as flowers. It is in vain that we point out the delicate traceries of frost on the sedums in the vertical rockery. She scowls, and curses all snowdrops, and heads indoors.

Actually I am sort of with her on snowdrops. In their simplest form they are charming objects. But some are double, and some gaze at the sky, and some are even pink. My late friend Patricia Cockburn, wife of Claud, the funniest journalist of the last century and Stalin's press officer at the Siege of Madrid during the Spanish Civil War, was a snowdrop fiend. Patricia took me to a special patch of her garden at Rock House in Ardmore, County Waterford, a village in which she competed for authority with the novelist Molly Keane. Here she showed me as weird a selection of galanthus as ever stopped a clock. There were double snowdrops, triple snowdrops, snowdrops turned inside out, and snowdrops in various pastel colours, including, as I remember, beige. I must have retched. She patted me sympathetically on the shoulder. 'Revolting, aren't they?' she said. 'But they're amazing swaps.' And she took me on another tour, this time of plants she had swapped for her disgusting snowdrops, including a beautiful *Rhododendron arboreum*, a myrtle possibly new to science, and an oak never before witnessed on land or sea.

The Duchess is out again, standing wrapped in a cloud of Capstan Full Strength smoke like a manifestation of Jehovah. The cloud speaks. It complains that there is an absence of decent smells. These would be provided, in the view of the Duchess, by wintersweet (planted ten years ago, not a sign of a flower yet) and *Hamamelis mollis* (never planted, too late now). Later we sit before the wheezing logs arguing about the purpose of scent in winter. I point out that your flower is seeking insects to pollinate it, and that given the extreme shortage of insects in temperatures around zero it is not amazing that the scents are on the hefty side. The Duchess starts sulking. She passes a note across to the effect that as far as she is concerned the whole bang shoot reeks of her erstwhile chauffeur's hair oil, and am I implying that she is some sort of damned bee? She then rises and leaves for the south of France. Good riddance, I think, as I open the windows and cart the gin bottles down to the bank.

But the place feels oddly empty now she is gone. It looks as gloomy as a fifteen-year-old's poem, black trees scratching a sky of lead with skeletal fingers, an angsty squish to every step you take on the lawn. The herbaceous plants lie in the border like burnt-out vehicles in the Iraqi desert. And the clouds press low from the north-west, yellowish-black like the smoke of burning oil wells. Dark wine. Early bed.

And next thing a brilliant light is knifing in, and it is seven in the morning, and it has snowed. The world is clean and new, and there are fox prints in line ahead, and rabbit prints two-abreast-and-two-ahead, and the merry cries of tinies from the slopes in the orchard. The Iraqi wrecks have festive snow hats on, and the seedheads of the *Eryngium horridum* have turned into space stations floating against the brilliant blue. And just as you are turning into a Schubertian Fotherington-Thomas who says hello sno hello sky I care not a row of buttons for your silly goles a garden is a love-som thing god wot, there arrives a really fine dose of *Schadenfreude*. Because when it started to fall the snow was wet. And the Leylandii hedge that has polluted the neighbourhood for the past thirty years, reaching a height of some sixty feet, got about a hundredweight of the stuff on every one of its branches. Upon which the trees just fell apart, and the whole works is nothing but a linear heap of firewood, and people have skied in from miles around to gloat.

But these are base thoughts, resembling the attitude of the ancient Roman climbing into the spatterproof toga prior to a really good lions *v.* Christians session in the Coliseum. As the slush gloom kicks in it is time to cleanse the soul with practicalities. The apple trees are in a shocking state, so it is time to take the middles out and get them organised. (Though actually goodness knows why. In the Marches the act of supreme politeness is *not* to offer your friends your apples in autumn. In return, your friends will refrain from offering you theirs, and everyone will deal with their own ton of fruit as seems best to them.) Figs need attention too; so we whimper as with freezing fingers we knock off the babies that would otherwise waste the energy we would wish the tree to expend on providing a decent crop late next summer.

For those who prefer the broad brushstrokes to the detail work, this is all a bit tedious. The reward lies at the end of the day, when the sky catches fire and the rooks whirl out of the trees like flakes of burnt paper, and the bonfire starts a plume green and thick and oily, then catches, *whoomp*, and you fork sides to middle until the stars peer down on a pile of grey ash. In which, unless you are a person of iron will, you will a couple of days later find yourself planting yet another ruddy apple tree.

And one day while we are out there, we will be much gratified to note that at noon the sun has managed to disentangle itself from the branches of the sugar maple. The year has turned. Can spring be far behind?

Absolutely miles. Time for another bonfire.

Wedding Fever

IT WAS A SHAKY BEGINNING to the year. Elderly relations kept ringing to say that because of the abominable things this ghastly government was doing the Gulf Stream was moving out to sea. Thank goodness (they said) there would be an election soon, if of course the thaw set in in time. At the time it was easy to believe this doomsaying. For months, all you could hear was the clatter of agriculturalists getting sugar beet out of the ground with road drills. There were many days when we looked out of the window at the snow-iced yews of the frozen Hope, and thought of the Azores, planted firmly in the Stream. The whole of the Azores is a garden. A farmer will plant a field of tea next to a field of potatoes. To separate the two, he will plant a row of hydrangeas. Then, recollecting that your hydrangea *en masse* can be a bit overwhelming, he will plant canna and madonna lilies on either side of the hydrangeas. Having stepped back to admire the effect against a background of blue sea and Ireland-green headland, he will then nip off and cook his lunch in a volcano.

But this is mere dreaming. We are in the Welsh Marches, not the Azores. We were beginning to panic when suddenly a warm blast swept in from the south-west, and the daffodils bowed their heads and blew their fanfares, and the birds started roaring away and building nests out of the straw with which we had been trying to protect the big-leafed hebes and the flowering sages.

Under normal circumstances, we would at this point have trudged around the garden admiring this and titivating that, and doing our best to effect last-minute pollination of the peach trees with the special dedicated hare's tail, and all the rest of it. But as the red tulips embarked on their annual race with the *Rheum atropurpureum* for the attention of the golden bamboo, our minds were on other things.

This is not a normal year. There is a wedding on, and the mighty resources of the Hope are focused on a single day in September. There have been debates about flowers.

There is a truck that occasionally parks in the small town just

45

down the road. This truck originates in a freight yard somewhere in the square miles of glasshouses that lie inland of the Hook of Holland. The writing on its side tells passers-by that it is run by Merry Pieter your Floral Friend. This charming nosegay of words cannot disguise the fact that it is a refrigerated lorry, its interior divided into chilly niches to resemble a mobile mortuary. In this columbarium repose the floral sweets of The Netherlands. At all seasons of the year there will be tulips black as Welsh steam coal, roses of a muddy bluish-red, bamboos tormented into the form of corkscrews, and *Salix tortuosa* in all the colours of the pastel rainbow. Some carping souls will say that these rare and delightful masterpieces of Baron Frankenstein's art have no smell. This is not true. The whole of the inside of the mortuary is pervaded with a light, refreshing aroma of disinfectant.

While this system represents a triumph of Dutch horticultural ingenuity, it does not chime with the desires of the bride-to-be, who is as sensible as she is beautiful. So we have decided as far as possible to Grow our Own. This will be no problem as far as roses go, because we will fill their roots with fish blood and bone and give them an extra hard prune and be totally conscientious about forcing weekend guests to do the deadheading before they are allowed any lunch. Oh, yes. The roses will, even in September, astonish us with their abundance, touch wood.

There are suggestions of chrysanthemums, but they are a bit too close to Merry Pieter's Funeral Specials. Dahlias are okay, though. I am aware that as a person of refined taste you are not supposed to grow these things, but we do it anyway, because George the Postman gives them to us.

Caroline Ede, Herefordshire's leading homegrown flower arranger, is very pro-dahlia for autumn weddings. She is also telling us to turn large tracts of the kitchen garden over to cosmos, and divisions of *Aster umbellatus*, and to be ready with zinnias, and to chop and line out bits of the rudbeckias in the borders. Personally, I view the use of the vegetable beds for cut flowers with the gravest suspicion. I mean, what are we supposed to eat? I have been arguing strongly for a bridal bouquet of spinach and curly kale, and vast arrangements of asparagus fern and globe artichokes, tremendously

festive. But I am a voice crying in the wilderness. So in they go,
zinnias last, because they hate a cold night. And I am taking it out
on the hydrangeas, pruned to two hefty shoots, and the *Clematis
orientalis*, which has been in the same place for uncounted years and
could certainly do with a feed. And Carrie seems happy, and so
does the bride.

We thought that the Duchess would not hold with all this
cottage-economy stuff. In her youth, relays of gardeners used to
appear from outlying estates, driving carts piled high with tube-
roses and hedychium and great mad swags of proteas. But you may
recall that she stumped out in the winter, leaving all the ashtrays
full and all the bottles empty. And on her return, she seems oddly
chastened. Apparently she has been staying with a friend who is an
ex-Minister of Defence in the Far East. She admires this person's
talent for arranging accidents for his political rivals. So naturally
she accompanied him on an official visit to Singapore, part of which
was a visit to the Botanic Garden. Here they showed her a lake that
contained thousands of turtles, each of whose shells was stencilled
with a Chinese character for good luck. Then they led her through
the Ginger Garden, heady with scent; so far so good. But finally
they took her to the Orchid Garden.

In this weird sanctuary, orchids are arranged in compositions
featuring chrome picture frames and synthetic tufa boulders. And
in a house she seemed to think was modelled on the pavilion at the
Generalife in Granada, she found herself among the Orchids of the
Famous, in which grow hybrids specially bred to celebrate international notables. There is 'Margaret Thatcher', who is a peculiarly
virulent puce with twiddly petals. Just down the row, the Duchess
claims, are 'Kim Jong Il' and 'Idi Amin'. And two along from Idi, she
said, a proud Malay hybridiser showed her something called 'The
Duchess', ivory white and slightly bloodshot. This may or may
not be true. Whatever the case, she was on the next plane home.

So she is being unusually helpful, and on we dig and delve. This
year even more than in most springs, in the general frenzy of work
it is hard to pay attention to what is happening here and now. But
there are moments when you can collapse by the pond and watch
the drift of kingcups do their sunshine-yellow thing, and the

gunneras unfold, and the bright regrowths of the dogwoods soften the brutality of their cut-back stumps. Meanwhile the divisions and the annuals shoot out of the ground, ready for duty. And here come the bees, droning their way into the kitchen garden. But they can buzz as hard as they like. They will not drown out the faraway strains of the organ in the church over the hill, for Mrs Preece is practising already. Here comes the bride, thrums the organ. At this rate she will need a machete to hack her way to the altar. But she's a good girl. She'll manage.

Being and Nothingness

A T LAST. At *last*. The dawn chorus is fading and a whiff of honeysuckle is creeping in at the window, mixed with a certain amount of sun. Outside, the dew hangs on the hedge, each drop a crystal ball. The future glimpsed within is that they will evaporate, and it will be another day that if not hot, will at least not require more than three jerseys. Summer, in short, is in our midst.

Naturally this has meant a frenzy of activity. The flowers for the wedding in September have got their heads well up, but no signs of budding yet, thank goodness. As soon as they do it will be time for the form of Chelsea Chop known as the Herefordshire Hack: a rose takes six weeks from zero to hero, so grit teeth, cling to holy relic and strike fearlessly with billhook. About the only part of the pleasaunces and messuages not down to late-flowering wedding gaudinesses is the pond. This is its usual dark and glassy self, if not a bit more so. We spent a cheerful few days in a canoe snipping away at dogwoods, which have now resprouted with commendable enthusiasm and are producing the usual bright variegations. We also removed several gargantuan water-lily roots, using the boat-anchor-attached-by-a-long-rope-to-the-tow-hitch-of-the-tractor method. The upside of this is that the water is beautifully clear and of a true obsidian darkness, in which the fish hang red-gold by the fringe of gunnera and water soldiers. The downside is that the shelter is much reduced, so various herons have decided that this is the avian equivalent of the baby food shelf in Boots.

Of course we cannot take this lying down. First we made a small raft, on which we placed a plastic owl. This looked horrible to all beholders except the herons, who ignored it. The same went for the CDs suspended overhead, and the orange electric fence round the edge. Someone else said we should erect multiple tripwires of monofilament fishing line, but all this did was disconcert the yellow wagtails whose job it is to contrast pleasingly with the goldfish. So in the end we settled for a wireless attached to a time switch that allows it to play in two-minute bursts between 4 a.m. and 8 a.m., by which time the household is making things too hot for herons. There are disadvantages. For one thing, it scares the hell out of the postman. For another, there is the debate about which programme herons like least. The World Service is pretty effective. The *Today* programme is not bad, particularly during an election. As for Radio 3's *Breakfast*, we rejected this on the grounds that not even herons deserve such a horrid blend of tweeness and musical lollipops, plus if we were caught the RSPCA would probably make us fill the pond in.

But it is several hours since John Humphrys mingled with the dawn chorus, and here we sit on the emerald lawn contemplating the darkness under the eaves of the wood. There is sun, there are shadows, and hammocks swing anywhere anyone can find a pair of trees. There is a measured swatting of wasps, and wafts of rose and tobacco, and the jingle of glasses as the sun goes down. It is all pretty mellow.

Too dashed mellow for the Duchess. She was subdued in the late spring, blaming something she had picked up in the Far East, though we suspected this was merely bad attitude. The other day she was leafing through her telegrams when she leaped to her feet. The Capstan went one way, the bottle the other. And suddenly all that remained of her was a cloud of smoke and a pool of gin soaking into the roots of the fremontodendron. An engine thundered in the drive. Round the corner of the yew hedge we saw the tail-light of her Norton Commando fishtail into the gloaming.

She was back the following week, practically bulging with strange oaths. Apparently she had been to a friend of hers in Notts, who was in charge of something called the Notional Thrust. The Thrust had been in the middle of acquiring a place called Crake Tower. The Duchess claimed with an odd vagueness to have spent sunlit weeks there as a girl. Over the days that followed, it all came out.

Crake (said the Duchess) was an English jewel. It sat in discreet Palladian magnificence at the centre of a vast landscape designed by 'Capability' Brown and improved by Repton. An earlier house had left traces, in the form of a parterre among whose hedgelets were patches not of coloured gravels, but of precious stones. Though most of these (said the Duchess, frowning sternly) had been swiped by beastly Communist gardeners, their sale having provided the seed finance for some of Britain's most vulgar garden centres. Flogging was too good for these people . . .

Someone gave her some gin. She drank deeply, then began again. The swallows were hawking busily over the reflecting pool, and a flycatcher was performing yo-yo evolutions from a base on the sculpture known as the Giant's Keyring, so it was hard to pay much attention. But out it all came, like glue from a jug. Beyond the parterre, apparently, were romantic walks lined with rhododendrons of surpassing rarity. There was a crinkle-crankle wall full of skep beehives. There were twin herbaceous borders a hundred yards long and ten yards deep, between which a path of ammonites led to a triumphal arch beyond which a Belfry of the Winds admired its reflection in a huge circular pond. The bell was rung at six every evening, said the Duchess, upon which enormous carp jutted their nebs through the lily-pads, awaiting delivery of loaves freshly baked in the Belfry's own kitchens. And behind the Belfry the Shropshire hills rose whaleback on blue whaleback.

'Hang on,' said someone. 'I thought we were in Nottinghamshire.' An airy wave of the Capstan left a lump of smoke tangled in the 'Zéphirine Drouhin'. Nottinghamshire, Shropshire, it seemed to say; who cared? The Duchess sat for a moment in her personal mushroom cloud, eyelids lowered in reverie. Then she started again, this time about the kitchen garden. Apparently there was forced seakale under crocks bearing the Crake crest, pineapples half-visible in the reeking steam of hotbeds.

Someone said they did not believe this place existed. Frankly, they spoke for us all.

The eyelids sank further, entirely masking the bloodshot orbs. The blue-veined hand carried the glass to the scarlet lips. The head shook, forbearing, patient. A garden in summer, said the Duchess in a low, weird voice, was a mingling of light and shade, plant and stone, opacity and translucence. But most of all it was a work of the human mind, without which none of the above attributes had any value, since they could not be perceived, let alone appreciated. Someone pointed out that this was all very well, but it left out great sheets of stuff like the smell of rose geraniums, the taste of green wine in the rain, the hope felt during the emergence of carrots, the grief inspired by the ring-barked maple, and above all a sense of the immediacy of the here and now. The Duchess muttered something about vulgar sensualists, and started to describe with Olympian detachment the parabolic curves of the Calculus Earthwork at Crake. At the end of this passage she lost her temper, asked me who the hell we thought we were, and pointed out that the Notional Thrust had already raised fourteen million pounds for the preservation and maintenance of Crake, which was not bad for a place that, all right, frankly, did not in fact exist. Gardens, said the Duchess, are better off not existing. Existence involves muck, weeding, and a lot of stuff that one wishes to do when one wants to, not when nature dictates – horrid stuff, nature, damn its impudence. Money is money, and much, much more important. Flowers fade. Money grows.

There was a general draining of glasses. The sun was dipping behind the cherries, striking bright gleams. 'Tell you what,' said someone. 'I am off to the greenhouse. I am going to pick about a stone of tomatoes. Of the stone, twelve pounds will be real and two pounds will be imaginary. You can choose your favourites from the imaginary ones. The rest of us will make the real ones into a salad.'

'Don't be so stupid', said the Duchess, salivating faintly.

The prosecution rests.

A Rich Filth

IT IS COLD, COLD, COLD. The hills look as if they have been dusted with icing sugar, and Dick the shepherd blows his nail on a full-time basis. Sensible creatures like woodlice and dormice are hibernating, and half the village, including the Duchess, is in the West Indies. But not us. Oh, no. All year we have been scheming modifications to the garden at the Hope. Now is the time to shake off the drowsiness of winter and surge ahead on many fronts.

There are the woods, for one thing. We started planting trees about twenty years ago, and have been at it ever since. The most recent excursion into silviculture has been in a derelict orchard stationed on a wettish north slope. An ash grove, we thought, how graceful, how plainly 'tis speaking, or would be if planted and given a chance. A hazel brake would also be good, and a couple of hundred walnuts, with a background of oak and wild cherry, these last being pretty much the weeds of our corner of the Welsh Marches. And how about some basket willows in the swampier bits?

So we planted the trees, and practically before you could blink the new ash had got its head above the bracken that infests the outlying corners, and the wonderful alchemy that turns a sour field into a rustling, odorous forest floor had begun. Late this autumn we got at the hazel with the coppicer's bow saw. While we were hacking our way through the glades, someone not in the working party fell into raptures about the branches and the sky and so on. We nodded and kept chopping. But when we went back to the house and set about the rare vintages, we began to discuss things. The new wood was all a bit, well, *drab*. A scheme began to form.

We put it into action without delay. Early the following morning we walked round the wood looking for vantage points, giving instructions to a half-frozen weekend guest holding a flag on a thirty-foot pole that represented a tree in twenty years' time. In spots determined by optimum flag visibility we stuck bamboos with labels attached. On the edge of the ash grove we planted a couple of manna ash, *Fraxinus ornus*. We studded the hazel margins with a clump of red-leaved cobnuts, and threaded the wild cherry plantation with Japanese blowsers, and put a black-leaved sycamore among the adventitious sycamores that had helicoptered in from the Park Wood, and stuck a couple of white-barked birches at the focal point of what we would maintain as a ride when we had put new piston rings in the tractor. We even started to talk musingly of rhododendrons. Recollecting ourselves with an effort, we fired up the chainsaws and hacked out slice vistas that directed the eye to rolling border hills and closed out the prospect of distant chicken sheds. Then we dusted our hands and stood back.

The wood looked as if it had recently formed part of the Battle of Ypres. Tree guards protruded from patches of raw earth like the grave-markers of the slain. It was time to go far away; like, for instance, to the kitchen garden, which has the merit of being at the opposite end of the policies.

There it lay, steaming faintly beneath its black sheets of woven plastic, except where the leeks and Aquadulce broad beans lurked in suspended animation under a light icing of snow. There were the polytunnels, two of them, misted with sweat. In their clammy vaults the Chinese leaves and red mustard were burgeoning, keeping the fearsome spectre of scurvy far from the household. Weeds were growing in the rows. These needed pulling out, though at this time of year the process induces in the icy-fingered puller a bitterness equivalent to several hundredweight of the worst radiccio. In the name of all that is cold and miserable, the puller thinks, what has induced us to extend the growing season into these dour and icy months? We should be hibernating, or at the very worst hanging out in a shed whose assets include an armchair and a retired blacksmith's forge.

There is no answer to this question. Throw the weeds on the frozen compost heap. It is time to contemplate the next assault on entropy.

Outside the south-west front of the house is a sunk garden. These words have been carefully chosen to imply high levels of grandeur, and mask rather than amplify the true state of affairs. The so-called sunk garden is a scruffy area of paving stones and gravel, with a bonfire pit, an appallingly rustic stone table and a rectangular pond that occasionally reflects sunlight into the low medieval room at its inner end. The wall round the sunk garden's margins holds a vertical rockery dedicated to sedums and sempervivums of various kinds, and a hefty population of weeds. Over this, emanating from a slightly raised bed, laps a charming flow of bigger alpines and hebes and one thing and another. At the top of the low wall at the bed's back, tree-studded lawns slide away into the eaves of the wood, slightly lifted by a plywood cutout of a giant boiled egg under an arch of yew.

Until the late summer there had never seemed to be any problem with this arrangement. Then a bunch of eastern Europeans turned up and erected a huge marquee on the lawn, and we had a wedding reception inside it. The wall of the marquee went up at the very margin of the sunk garden. And it became apparent that said sunk garden, far from being a sort of no-man's-land between lawns and house, was actually a deeply charming area, instinct with horticultural potential. The reason this idea had come into being was that the tent wall stopped the eye, persuading it to concentrate on the stuff close at hand rather than wander off into the woods.

After discussion, we decided that it would not be sensible to get the marquee back. It would cost too much, for one thing. For another, the first one killed most of the lawn, and the younger members of the family like a game of cricket from time to time. Furthermore the pressure to have a couple of hundred people to dinner most weekends would be hard to resist. A plant-based solution suggested itself. We would put in a hedge round the top of the sunk bit to give an illusion of containment, leaving gaps or embrasures through which the eye could wander to specially selected targets like the Huge Boiled Egg and its companion sculpture the Giant's Keyring. But what would the hedge be made of? Yew, of course, said the usual voices.

The whole place is studded with yews, and a long, slow journey they have been, I said. Fine, they grow nine inches a year, but of course you have to cut that nine inches back by six inches, which makes the annual increment three inches, and we will have to plant them at two-foot intervals, and have you any idea how much all that will *cost*? Plus it will look ghastly for the first five years, and what do you think we are, Hungarian peasants who live to be a hundred and thirty thanks to a diet of yoghurt and the pollen of Carpathian bees? What? Morbid? Me? Oh, all *right*.

So in it goes, the fortress wall of yew. For the moment we have enlisted the help of Jenny Crisp, whose powers of wattling are astounding. She is going to teach us to weave hazel and willow from the woods into complex rhythmic patterns to make a temporary fortification while the yews grow. Behind the wattle the dark-green wall will rise. Morbid thoughts will be held at bay. We will draw strength from the example of the great J. C.Williams of Caerhays in Cornwall. As a young man he bred daffodils. In early middle age he turned his attention to rhododendrons. Late in life he proceeded to magnolias, many of which had no plans to flower until they had been forty years in the ground; and he ended his days while still engaged in a controlled burst of oak planting.

Oh, yes. We will wait for a bit of a thaw. Then we will plant eighteen-inch yews in a rich filth. Then, finally, like all sensible creatures, we will give way to drowsiness and hibernate. If we can fit it in before the tulips arrive.

Beware! Spring!

THE TIDE OF WINTER took its time about ebbing this year. It rose very high, and it battered the garden at the Hope with rough blue waves of frost. We crouched in the parts of the house least accessible to the elements, swathed in down-filled garments that looked like lifejackets, trying to breathe life into a lemon verbena someone had left in a shed. The patient died, and we stomped around the place kicking things and making short dashes for firewood. We paid unnecessary attention to last year's cuttings, frozen out of the cold frame and onto the kitchen windowsill. We listened religiously to the weather forecast, heartbeat accelerating at any hint of relief; behaving, in short, in the neurotic manner of horticultural Robinson Crusoes, marooned on an island of above-zero in a limitless ocean of cold. Then one day the air softened, and woodpeckers were clattering on their hollow trees, and a blackbird cleared its throat and had a preliminary tootle from a beak that matched the crocuses under the mulberry tree. It was time to go out, survey the wreckage, and salvage what we could.

First of all there were the bodies to burn. A couple of ceanothus were black and frozen, and the non-variegated red sage was a goner. We had swathed the variegated sage in horticultural fleece, and done the same for the myrtle. All winter they had hung around, ghostly in the rain, lumpy in the snow, tatterdemalion in the gales. When I unpacked them, the sage was as cheerful as could be expected, but the myrtle was a grim dead brown. What, I said to myself, did you expect? Myrtles are apparently a sign that there have been Quakers on the place, and you are an admirer of Quakers, not a Quaker. I contemplated hauling the whole dismal apparatus out of the ground, but I lacked the will. Shaking my head, I went on my gloomy way.

To tell the truth, there was not a lot else to be gloomy about. As usual one of our neighbours has decided to put down a ludicrously huge number of pheasants. This is nice for us in the winter, as the freezer is now full of them. It is also pleasant in early spring. I have already mentioned that the pheasants of my infancy were drab creatures, well adapted for slinking around unperceived. I say 'pheasants'; actually I should say 'pheasant', as the one I remember best was a solitary creature who lurked morosely in the ilexes that stood between the house and the North Sea. We ended up calling him Dave, and chasing him round the wood with our little shotguns while he laughed at us sardonically from behind a tree.

Your modern Marcher pheasant looks as if he has nipped down to Mappin and Webb for a quick going-over before returning to mix it with the hens. The body glows a burnished orange-copper, the ring round the neck is silvery white, and the eye glares from the iridescent head, illuminated by the purest stupidity. These are not wild game birds, but edible garden ornaments. They and their wives have trampled the beds picking up spare seeds from the bird feeders, and will now vanish into the undergrowth for a bit of hanky panky. Good riddance, because they clash with the tulips.

The golden bamboo is another matter. All winter long it stood calm and splendid. Then a particularly swingeing frost scalped it. Now it looks scruffy, but alive. We gave it a word of cheer, wishing it a hot, wet growing season and a total absence of pandas, and passed on to the maples. These are in terrific shape, having brushed off the winter chill with a light shrug and festooned themselves with emerging leaves like small red shrimps.

Oh, yes. The mood is getting lighter all the time, ably assisted by the Riot of Colour. The Yew Teeth at the front of the house are now a fair size, and clipped into square pegs. Their winter job is to look snow-capped and menacing. Their spring job, which they are now doing, is to rise from merry gums of polyanthus, the more colours the better. The wallflowers are emitting their charmingly frowsy hum on the Beach, and the Scrap Border is beginning to do its duty. There are hyacinths, and primroses, and crocuses, and early tulips, and squills, and anything else that might respond to interment, and when they get to flowering it is like the early stages of a two-day migraine. Tch, cry visitors of the greenery-yallery persuasion, what vulgarity! But the Duchess is back from Mustique, tanned as an old shoe, and unless she gets a good dose of colour into her eyes the expense in Plymouth gin will be more than we can handle. Once the greenery-yalleries catch sight of her, or rather the Capstan

Full Strength burning a charred groove beside all the others on the
library windowsill, they go strangely quiet and express a wish to
view segments of the far policies in which it is not conceivable that
they have any interest at all.

The above is a long way of saying that she is back, and will need
feeding. The fatted calf has been whimpering in its straw for weeks,
but it is okay, because by the way Her Grace is roaring for sweet
potatoes it is reasonable to assume that she has gone vegetarian.
Some people can apparently grow sweet potatoes in Marcher green-
houses. At the Hope, we reckon that life holds enough suffering
without that kind of carry-on. The nearest we come to tropical is
a bit of Japanese mustard under plastic; and unfortunately these
salads, charming in early March, are now reached a stage of rank-
ness where only strong boiling makes them edible. So it is out to the
kitchen garden, and prepare the beds, and get the Arran Pilots in,
and try to decide what to do with the artichoke bed, swept clean
by -20° Centigrade. And all of a sudden the Duchess is merely the
distant sound of a sea shanty, and the rush is on.

There is rotavating, and hoeing, and wholesale removal of stones,
and the dribbling of seeds down grooves in the ground. There is a
quick dash to St-Pol-de-Léon to collar offsets of the only kind of
artichokes worth growing. There is a wholesale pruning of roses,
and planting of lilies, and hacking back of tree peonies so they
produce lots of nice leaves and who cares about the boring yellow
flowers, and cutting of pea sticks from hazel stools. There is no
moment's peace between dawn and dusk, and even then we live in
perpetual terror of a late frost sending its nasty white fingers out
of the mountains and frizzling the little green tendrils of spinach.
There is also, it must be admitted, a furtive application of Roundup
to the asparagus bed; as a result of which the asparagus is beat-
ing the couch grass out of the ground for the first time in living
memory. We hate doing it, but plead *force majeure*. Even the Duchess
can be made to behave by the first asparagus of the season.

So here we are. Everything is green and humming. The swallows
are back in the barn. Dawn is early, but we wake up with it because
the birds are shouting in at the window. Now that everything is
growing, we have the courage to go and heave out the wrecks so

we can replant the spots left naked. Out of the ground and onto the bonfire they go. And finally, it is the myrtle's turn. The executioner trudges grimly towards the condemned shrub, pickaxe in hand – Wait!

At the base of the wreck, something is happening. There are little heart-shaped leaves, and they are green, not brown. The myrtle lives! Spring is in the step, and in the air. All over the place, in fact.

The Duchess Returns

THERE ARE NO WEDDINGS this year, or at least none in the immediate family. Just as well, really. The spring drought caused a sort of motorway pile-up in the garden. The daffodils were out at the same time as the tulips, the lilacs, and several roses of the climbing persuasion. On going out to pollinate the peaches with the ceremonial hare's foot, we were practically blinded by a cloud of Red Admirals. These then settled on the *Malus transitoria*, which has grown into the *M. spectabilis* in the Crab Orchard, producing an effect not unlike a medium-sized galaxy in which someone has left the Christmas lights on. This distracted our attention from the corpses, of which there were several. The mats of South African daisies were putrid and hopeless, the yuccas were knackered and the golden bamboo was sere and beige.

We adjusted. The peaches set, and the blossoms fell off, and the click of the croquet ball was heard in the land. The odd shower arrived – I refer to the weather, not the cousins who came to stay in a steady stream. The last cousin left. Some crates of pink wine arrived in a van. It became possible to do something useful for a change. Just as we were drawing up some deckchairs to the pond with a view to counting the number of mutant goldfish, a London taxi drew up with a crunch of gravel. There was a fierce burst of invective and the Duchess got out and stumped into the house, leaving us to carry in four trunks and pay the bill, which amounted to £796.20 plus tip.

Her Grace had a slightly flayed look, which led us to believe that she had probably been deprived of an ozone layer, which meant Antarctica. There was of course no actual confirmation of this, since she went straight from the taxi to her bed, where she remained for some days. The only sign of her presence was the occasional Plymouth gin bottle arcing out of her window and curt notes asking someone to unblock the washbasin in her bathroom, which on inspection proved to be bunged up with Capstan Full Strength butts.

Finally she came down wearing a filthy towelling dressing gown

bearing the words HOTEL MAGNIFICO USHUAIA – DO NOT
REMOVE and dived into the library. Certainly Antarctica, we said
to each other, wagging our heads in the manner of those seeking to
inflate a small truth to obscure a great disaster.

Soon, notes began slithering under the library door. Some of
these were merely administrative, demanding further supplies of
gin, cigarettes and relations to bully. Others were specific requests.
One, for instance, said I WANT AN ICEBERG. We do not, of
course, grow Iceberg lettuces in the garden, but some rather delicious Little Gems had just come into heart, and we sent her one
of those. Quick as a flash another note came back. A REAL ONE,
MORON, it said. Of course she had locked the library door, but
we spent quite a long time explaining through the keyhole that
icebergs were impractical, and that just as Norfolk's clouds are its
mountains, the icebergs of the Welsh Marches are in fact its wild
cherry woods, whose blossoms she had missed because she had
been faffing about in the Southern Hemisphere at the time.

This explanation was rather distractingly interrupted by the
sound of glass breaking in a stone fireplace. We waited, breathless.
Sure enough another note slid under the door. A PENGUIN THEN,
it said. So it was down to the local Rare Breeds establishment on
the trail of the domestic penguin.

There was a coruscating spectrum of domestic fowls. There were
Andalusians, Peking Bantams, and some objects that looked as if
they had been bred to clean chimneys. Not a sniff of a penguin,
though. Things were looking difficult. Then someone suggested
ringing up Jeff Koons, purveyor of giant floral animals to the international cognoscenti.

Jeff Koons' galérienne, an exceptionally refined type of person,
seemed put out that anyone had asked her for anything. Still, she
said with a slight sniff, Jeff could probably fit in a forty-foot floral
penguin for about ten million as long as we did not mind waiting six
or seven years. She might have been about to say more, but there
was no way of knowing, since an involuntary movement of the arm
had torn the telephone out of the wall.

By this time the sound of breaking glass was constant, and
the smell seemed to indicate that the Duchess was smothering

furniture fires with a set of Audubon's *Birds* to which we have for some reason formed a sentimental attachment. People weeding the Japanese anemones under the library window were bringing back a succession of notes saying things like PENGUIN NOW OR THE CARPET GETS IT. Desperate measures were indicated. And, since the versatile gardener is not a procrastinator, taken.

It took several days in the Royal Horticultural Society's library. The summer sun beat down on the pavements of Vincent Square and back into our eyes. We dismissed from our minds thoughts of the pale shade of the Himalayan whitebeam, under which we could have been inhaling Château de Sours. We researched, made drawings, came home, trundled the cement mixer out of the garage, rented diggers, dumpers and dozers, and alerted an elite corps of local growers. We bid a fond farewell to the Mount in the Stuart Plock, and moved in.

In the great days of rock gardening, the cognoscenti used to make replicas of Mont Blanc. If they could make a mountain with rock plants, we reasoned, we could make an iceberg with bedding. So we confected a jagged lump of earth and rocks, and on its slopes and crags we planted a sheet of mesembryanthemums and one thing and another. A couple of showers, and there it was, gleaming white. Then we got hold of Henry Stanhope from down the road, a gap-year youth of good family with the enormous Stanhope nose, and paid him minimum wage to stand on top of the thing all day wearing a dinner jacket. Frankly the whole performance looked like the wrath of God, but anything to stay on the right side of the Duchess, whom we now summoned from the library.

She came. She saw. She said, 'That's not a real penguin,' by which we concluded that she had been deceived by the iceberg. Then she went back into the house.

The library door was open. We went in and shovelled out the bottles and sent Audubon for rebinding and did what we could with the carpet. By the time we had finished it was evening, and the sun was pouring through the trees like golden syrup. Bathed in the rays at a green plastic table sat the Duchess, with her back to the iceberg. She was sniffing at a strand of Japanese honeysuckle, and her eyes were narrowed at a gap between the dogwoods, beyond which the valley of the Arrow faded into the far blue haze. We poured her a glass of wine and hid our surprise when she refused a Capstan Full Strength. Someone asked if she liked her iceberg.

'What iceberg?' she said, and the big rubies on her ring glittered as she rolled the honeysuckle.

'And the penguin?'

'What penguin?'

'Quite so,' we said. Then we went and fired Henry. Next day we turned the iceberg back into the Mount, and it was summer. The Duchess is weeding, rings and all. There are a hundred and forty-six goldfish in the pond, nineteen of them with the sought-after triple tail. Things are pretty much back to normal, and about time too.

All at Sea

THE BREEZE IS SIGHING in the flaming maples, and the ground is steady underfoot. There is leaf mould and wood smoke in the air. We are on dry land again. It is not exactly a relief, because the sea is a splendid spot, except when it is trying to drown you. But the lawns are mown, and the trees are doing their autumn stuff, and the sedums have been at it for some time. Which certainly makes a change.

Let me explain.

I am writing a book about the gardens of the western seaboard of the British Isles – large-scale slabs of paradise spreading from Abbotsbury round the Lizard to St Michael's Mount and Tresco, and on up the west of Ireland, and even, in grown-out and jungly form, behind Clough Williams-Ellis's folly-village at Portmeirion. They continue up the coast of Scotland, petering out only at Inverewe, immaculate under the eyes of the Great Northern Divers peering through its gates, on the same latitude as Moscow.

The Scottish gardens are generally best seen before July. There are a couple, however, to which the seasons make little difference. Which explains why we were sailing in a small boat across the Sea of the Hebrides, in which the occasional porpoise was rolling, and across whose western horizon lay a tangle of mountains festooned with inky swags of cloud: the island of Rum.

The story of Rum is on the peculiar side. As far as I can make out, it belonged in the nineteenth century to Lord Salisbury, who occasionally stalked its red deer and otherwise adopted in its regard one of the great Victorian attitudes he personified, viz. laissez-faire. Rum already had a heaped dose of the other, viz. splendid isolation. Salisbury seems to have tired of the island, and sold it to someone called Campbell, who rented it to John Bullough, an inventor of weaving machinery, who bought it and left it to his son George. George duly inherited a vast fortune, the size of which was equalled only by his enthusiasm for spending it.

With a view to this, he commissioned a 120-ft steam yacht, the

Rhouma, in which he sailed round the world, befriending en route
the Emperor of Japan, who presented him with some rare plants
and a number of home decor items in the Buddho-Gothic taste. On
arriving once more in home waters, Bullough decided that the Sea
of the Hebrides was the perfect spot for a holiday home. He therefore caused to be built on Rum, an island made of fine and obdu-
rate granite, a house of red sandstone that he brought by freighter
from Annan in Dumfriesshire. This bulky and threatening edifice
is known as Kinloch Castle. In it he installed the Emperor's phoe-
nixes and dragons, and also (among other modern conveniences) an
Orchestrion or automatic organ, and a billiard room from which the
cigar smoke was removed by a system of forced draughts. He also
changed the island's name to Rhum, which sounded more Hebridean, and did not constitute an inducement to strong drink; though
many pointed out, rightly, that never mind the name, the climate
of the place would drive you to drink if it was called Narnia or
Tooting Bec.

Naturally there was plenty to do in the horticultural line. Bullough laid out a walled garden of some five acres. He imported a
quarter of a million tons of soil, installed a Japanese bridge over a
burn, made plantings of wet-weather exotics, trees, and presumably the botanical gifts of the Emperor of Japan. He attached to the
house at least one conservatory, for use on days when Rum's midges
made outdoor life impossible. Actually it sounds more like a stove,
since its pools were home to a selection of alligators, and humming-
birds flitted among the orchids.

Little evidence of the garden remains. Rum is a remorseless spot.
Its red deer, deprived of vital minerals, have turned carnivorous.
Its weather, funnelled down the glen at the eastern end of which
Bullough's house stands, is exceptionally fierce. Gardeners on the
western fringe of things need to plant windbreaks. Tresco's took
thirty years and the introduction of the Monterey pine to get prop-
erly established; Inverewe's is founded on remnants of the Caledonian forest. The Kinloch windbreak is hefty and tangled now,
but in its early years it failed to do the job. One gale apparently
plucked the conservatory from the side of the house, alligators and
all, and dumped it in a distant spinney. Soon after that, Bullough

lost interest. The dozen men who had toiled in the garden were disbanded, and the weeds crept in from the wilderness and met in the middle, and the First World War swept the taste for such extravagances into the dustbin of history.

Bullough's widow left the place to the Scottish nation, on condition that none of its contents be moved from the island. The house and its sandalwood dragons and damask sofas rotted, and the Orchestrion was attacked by woodworm. The walls of the garden tottered, and the government took over. The Prince's Trust helped with a campaign for the house's restoration, and the Japanese bridge was rebuilt in steel. Now, the garden is a tangled morass, in which strands of fuchsia struggle with ivy, and dells and rills are mere dips in the Hebridean rainforest.

To get into the kitchen garden where the men laboured to bring fruit and vegetables and cut flowers to readiness for Bullough's annual three weeks, you thread a chicane of security fencing festooned with safety warnings. There is a polytunnel, with enfeebled cabbage seedlings. At the back of the house a plumber is drinking strong Czech lager at three in the afternoon. It is still a wild and beautiful place, with exciting gothic overtones. It is also a good example of what can happen when an island garden goes wrong.

A dozen-odd miles of angry sea to the northwest is Canna, a brilliant green hump of orchid-studded turf looking west towards the Outer Hebrides. There is a harbour on Canna, safe in all weathers. Houses are scattered over the green turf, and there are three churches. If all the churches were consecrated, they would have a congregation of between five and seven each. Two, however, are no longer active. One, a remarkably beautiful structure in the Celtic tradition, is a good place to sit, and has a large, splendid escallonia over its gate. The other deconsecrated church was built in the neo-Romanesque-Byzantine-Damn-the-Expense style by the Marquis of Bute. He adopted the Bullough kit form technique, bringing the stone from elsewhere, ready cut for assembly. The ship left the materials on the site and sailed away. Up went the church and down went the congregation. About ten years ago it became a Hebridean research centre. Water streamed in, gravely prejudicing the research materials within. Finding myself talking to the

architect in charge of the conversion at a party in Oxfordshire, I
mentioned that the roof seemed to leak incurably. 'Not the roof,'
said the architect. 'The walls.'

'Walls?' I said.

'Canna,' said the architect wearily, 'was an island of crofters.
Under all that beautiful green turf lies a soil far too acid to be
convenient. What would you do if you were a crofter and someone
landed thirty tons of lime on the beach and left it lying around till
the masons arrived?

They had nicked, apparently, the lot. The Marquis's church is
built on sand.

There is a big (but not too big) house on Canna, once inhab-
ited by the Gaelic scholar John Lorne Campbell, an enlightened
landlord whose widow died aged a hundred and one in 2004. It
sits behind a screen of sycamores, their leaves salt-blasted to the
texture of elephants' ears, and remnants of a garden, with an escallonia tunnel leading to the front door from the gate on the bright
rotten-granite road. The school, now mothballed for lack of pupils,
has made a museum in one of the potting sheds. Rabbits tunnel
under unpruned roses and among ragged lines of vegetables. It is
supposed to be a community garden. But the inhabitants of Canna
must have enough to do without maintaining surplus acres. Perhaps
these oases perched on the western rim of the habitable world need
to be autocracies not only in their foundation but in their continu-
ation. Autocracy or democracy, though, a late gale can still scupper
you.

They are melancholy places in early autumn, these struggling
gardens. The boats lie in the harbour while the gales scream by,
and the salt-scorched branches thrash overhead as you walk down
the wet road weighed down by a sense of the futility of human
effort. But as you look east down the harbour of Rum the dawn is
rising over the land in a sea of blood; and as you crouch in the roar
of Canna House's escallonia tunnel a ray of sun is drawing a golden
carpet across the sea.

One day the wind dropped and we sailed home. Where we picked
the last of the roses, and admired the single chrysanthemums and

the last of the Michaelmas daisies, very small and cloud-like, nothing as vulgar as a colour. Any minute now all the leaves will be off. The potatoes are in bags, and the apples in the sheds, and the walnuts pickled in their jars. There are miles of woods between us and the sea; the salty gales cannot touch us here. Which is a pity, in a way. Still. In with the firewood, and out with the books and the wine, and down, down, into the cold black winter.

Not Just the Weather

WINTER CAME EARLY this year, in a manner that would perhaps have evoked nostalgia in persons displaced from yurts in the Gobi. Assisted by an almost total lack of rain, the leaves started falling off the trees in September. Friends arriving from Sussex, normally offensively smug and deeply bronzed after a long, hot season, paused only to wring out their socks before beginning to moan about the wettest summer ever. We shook our heads in sympathy and said we were sorry for their trouble. A blast of wind blew the last of the leaves into the puddle formerly known as the horse pond; and there we were, rumbling down the year's ramp into a dry black pit of winter.

I realise at this point I am talking about the weather, which is (the Duchess says, and I agree) a tedious thing to do, and unilluminating. I shall however persist. This is not the pathetic fallacy, in which emotion and climate march in lockstep to enhance the dramatic effect of doubtful novels. With a garden as an intermediary, the weather has a real and powerful effect on the emotions. Things at the Hope were frankly dire. Expanses of dust spread away in all directions, whipped into choking clouds by icy breezes. Most things not dried up had fallen over. It got to the Duchess fast. She is still technically on the wagon and off the Capstan Full Strength, but she finds desiccation and collapse depressing. We do not like to admit this even to ourselves, but there are times when she lurches into the drawing room smelling like a leaky distillery. Furthermore, the parts of her fingers visible between the diamonds have taken on a brownish hue. In this weather, the bronzing is more likely to be nicotine than suntan, and her attempts to disguise it by weeding are fooling nobody, since most of the weeds have died of drought.

Still, life must go on. We put the garden more or less to bed, hurling muck around in all directions, covering the vegetable department with black plastic and making little dressing-gowns of horticultural fleece for the borderline hardy stuff – once bitten twice shy, and last winter made shocking holes in the borders.

We gave the yews a final high-sensitivity nip, shoved a Nicorette prescription bearing the number of the local AA branch under the Duchess's door, and made for Palermo. This sounds as if we go to Palermo all the time. Not the case. Indeed I had read so many descriptions of Palermo's civic brutishness and private thuggery that it was about the last place I wanted to go. Still, those in the know speak highly of the botanical gardens there, and a free ticket is a free ticket, so off we went.

The beginning was frankly something of a cliché. The hotel itself was in a respectable part of the town, next to the armoured glass façade of a bank. Someone had tried to enter the bank by blowing the doors in with a double-barrelled shotgun, the marks of whose buckshot remained in the glass. This induced a rather Godfather-ish mood, and we started talking out of the side of the mouth and not telling each other where we were going for lunch on the grounds that it might incriminate us. The Botanic Garden, however, fixed all this. In a frankly second-rate city, the Botanic Garden is a first-rate thing. Its splendid collection of trees begins almost at the entrance, with a multi-trunked *Ficus magnolioides* whose like I have only seen previously in Honolulu, and continues for hectare after blessed hectare.

As we stood admiring it the sky turned the colour of blue-black Quink, and thunder banged immediately overhead. We cowered under a cheap umbrella. A thicket of skyscraping Indonesian bamboos looked completely at home, its leaves living William Morris wallpaper, its trunks golden pillars as fat as your leg. A bamboo person once told me that bamboos unfold like telescopes from the stool, growing at three feet a day. In Palermo in the downpour, they seemed to be unlimbering as we watched.

There is a lot of marvellous stuff here, all of it exotic to the northern eye but none of it outlandish. Particularly winning is the habit of displaying a huge range of a single species in large earthenware pots. We had previously seen this only in William Waterfield's garden in Menton, where he uses it to show to good effect his remarkable collection of pygmy gladioli. In Palermo, they use the system for cacti. On and on they went, rank after rank of globes and organ pipes and amorphous objects like spiny clouds, each in its elegant red pot, ready to be moved indoors should the weather turn inclement. We were entirely lost in the spiny topography of cactus world when a harsh voice croaked from a dripping arbour that it was closing time, and we should leave.

This was a lie, signifying only that the shouter was getting bored and wanted to go home early. We walked into the library and lecture theatre, designed in the late 1780s by Léon Dufourny, French author of *The Diary of a Jacobin in Sicily*, and an architect under the somewhat barmy influence of his idealist compatriots Boullée and LeDoux. LeDoux designed buildings adapted carefully to their purpose, such as a waterkeeper's house with the rooms built into the thickness of an enormous drainpipe through which a river flowed. Boullée is perhaps most famous for a design for a Tomb for Newton, in which the great natural philosopher's sarcophagus lies on the bottom of an enormous sphere pierced to simulate the constellations by day, and lit at night by a vast lamp which simulates the sun.

Not very astonishingly, neither of these designs was built. Dufourny, however, had better luck. His answer to the need for an interpretive hub for the Palermo Botanic Garden is a structure in the Egypto-Graeco-Romano-*Droits-de-l'Homme*-Cecil-B-deMille taste. Its twin merits are that it is an amusing building of considerable grandeur, and that its pediment is a good place to stand in a downpour and contemplate the fact that this was the first garden in Europe to see the loquat and the mandarin.

We then travelled elsewhere in Sicily, but found little in the way of gardens. Vineyards, yes, and shade trees, and spiky-leaved objects whose true nature was obscured by cloud pruning; but no actual gardens. Perhaps this is not surprising, as by this time we were on a boat, sailing, eating at night in small restaurants where there always seemed to be one table over which presided a man with cold eyes to whom all the other men at the table would defer. And we saw something else: something terrible. Bear with me.

We sailed on to Malta. Malta is big on glacis, revetments, machicolations and Piranesian immensities, but it is remarkably short on trees and shrubs, except for a splatter of public gardens studded with plaques commemorating dozens of British seamen drowned while yachting. A sombre mood had set in. This was partly due to the drownings and the stone. But there was also something else.

Before we had sailed from Sicily we had dined in a grim little restaurant in a town called Gela, a famous Mafia stronghold dominated by a vast oil refinery. The man in the place of honour at the long table at the end of the restaurant had glanced up. He was smiling, but his eyes were cold and glabrous as crude oil. A figure sitting opposite him, washing sea urchins down with fierce draughts of grappa, rose and slid out of the room, casting a swift glance over her shoulder as she left. The glance had been enough. *The woman was the Duchess.*

In the armoury of the Royal Palace in Malta, where a charming garden of hibiscus and oleander stands guard over a fine collection of implements designed to cause agony and death, all these influences made us finally decide we had had enough. We rushed to the airport, boarded a plane, and made our way through cloud, fog and ice back to the Hope.

The red dogwoods were blazing over the pond, which was fuller than any we had seen in Sicily. White frost silvered the yews, the woodpecker was on the Giant's Keyring, and if you lay down and looked up, you were gazing straight into the wild brindlings of a hellebore. The smell was moss and mould and must, like a tabletop of medlars; and into it was mixed a faint whiff of wood smoke.

At the sound of wheels on the drive the front door opened, and there was the Duchess. Her eyes gleamed with health, and when we kissed her, she smelled faintly of Chanel and apple logs; no hint of Capstan. 'Where have you been?' she said.

'Sicily.' I thought of the restaurant, and shivered. 'Do you by any chance know anyone who lives there?'

'My brother,' she said, and shook her head. 'Lives in a place called Gela. Ghastly place. Ghastly man. Won't be going there again in a hurry. Glad you're back.'

'Us too,' I said. Winter at the Hope? Can't beat it.

Before the Storm of Spring

IT HAS BEEN AN ODD YEAR SO FAR. I suspect the international situation may be a touch on the grave side, as someone from the *Tatler* rang up the other day and asked for instructions on how to skin a rabbit. I told him, and he thanked me on behalf of his readers, and my thoughts returned to a less frantic channel, viz. the one that leads to willows.

How we do like a willow. In the land of orange trees it mimics an orange. In Arctic spots it grows over rocks in a furtive manner, keeping its head down as the blizzards howl out of the leaden horizon. At the Oval it makes a charming bat. And at the Hope it grows like a weed, in large numbers and many varieties.

It is possible to trace the origins of this affection. A few years ago I was given a tour of his National Collection by Christopher Newsholme, became possessed by the versatility of the species and drove home with a bundle of sticks under my arm. Sections of the Hope are a bona fide upland swamp. Assisted by the outflow from a rogue cesspit, these spots provided perfect ground for the striking and subsequent burgeoning of said sticks. Pretty soon, under the influence of Jenny Crisp, we were harvesting the one-year wands of *Salix viminalis* and using them to make stuff.

Not elaborate stuff, you understand. No Wicker Men. Not even the Crisp-style weaving of split shoots through iron railings to soften their Victorian grimness. All we have done is bang some big stakes into the ground and weave wands through them in a rough alternation. From a distance it looks like a wattle hurdle on a Brobdignagian scale. From close up it looks like the wrath of God.

But I do not care, because we were following a plan.

In this corner of the garden, which greets the visitor as soon as he drives into the yard, there was once a barrier handcrafted in traditional Marcher style from a few sheets of corrugated iron nailed onto some disused railway sleepers. Naturally the tin proved an affront to the delicate sensibilities of the inhabitants. So we tore it down and planted a 'Paul's Himalayan Musk' – a cutting of one that used to grow up the Dower House at Stanton Lacey and therefore a vegetable of high sentimental value. We then stood back and allowed nature to take its course. Within four years it had become obvious that unless something was done the only way we would ever find the barn again was with a dowsing rod and some dynamite.

Luckily this conclusion coincided with a weekend on which many people were staying. We took a chain and attached one end to the long-suffering tractor. The other end we sent into the heart of the rose, carried by a youth famous for his powers of rapid healing. He attached the chain to the rose's central trunk and emerged bleeding but triumphant. The tractor driver drove away, towing the rose out of the ground. We buried it in a distant corner of the policies, where it has ever since constituted a scented pinkish-white fountain for a single week in June and an affront to health and safety for the rest of the year.

This left us with a crater and nothing much to do with it. The Duchess then piped up, claiming she had an idea. Why, she said, would we not have one of those charming live-willow fences, which would in time grow into a sort of thornless zareba against all those ghastly hawkers and circulars and people who were always nipping round to drink her drink?

I pointed out that it was important to get out of the place occasionally, if only to renew the stocks of gin and Capstans to which she was at that time a slave. My secret thought, of course, was that it was bad enough having to keep the lawn mown without having to control willows growing three foot a week in the season, never mind the damage they could do to the main drain as it sidles past the barn. Infinitely preferable (I said) to do a bit of wattling.

She told me that I knew nothing about wattling, and of course she had a point. But when we lived in Ireland I spent a goodish amount of time with two kind basket makers who occupied a cottage by the banks of the river Blackwater at Mallow. These men sat on kitchen chairs with the legs sawn off in a room that I seem to remember was floored with about six inches of water. All day they wattled away, discussing topics of current significance and scarcely looking at the beautiful fishing creels and oyster baskets they turned out without apparent effort. Wattling could not, I thought, be too difficult.

Which just shows how wrong you can be. We cut some wands, drove some stakes into the ground and got weaving. The first attempt looked like Shredded Wheat under high magnification. We had another go. The Duchess marched to and fro shaking her head and spitting rogue bits of tobacco into the pond. I knew that unless I made an intelligent suggestion eftsoons or right speedily, I was going to be unweaving the second attempt and rewattling like a hedge sparrow. I therefore observed that not all roses are as rampant as your 'Paul's Himalayan Musk', placed an order with David Austin, and planted the polite yellow objects that arrived hard against the wattling.

And up they came. I was struck by the sight of them the other morning, in their third year, making a bright and civil lattice where once the shredded wheat loured accusingly across the pond. The willow, it seems, has more or less rotted away, and the roses support themselves. Which is just as I had hoped, though when I am discussing this kind of thing with the Duchess I substitute for the word 'hope' the word 'intended'.

It is possible that this is enough about willows. But they resemble peanuts in the respect that once you get started on them, it is hard to stop.

It was a tough late winter in the garden, and cutting the willow wands was only part of it. The winds were high, the temperatures low, and the only way we got through the willow-cutting weekend was to listen to the *Histories of Tacitus* on the earphones which are now a constant companion for the more tedious tasks about the place. The bloody deeds of the Emperors after Nero are highly conducive to hack and slash – I seem to remember that the decapitation of Licinianus had a particularly invigorating effect while pollarding. But there came a day when all the winter stuff was done, and the shallots were turning into little green fountains, and the crows were showing an interest in the Aquadulce beans that meant something was stirring down there in the mud.

Soon after this I was bringing in a load of logs. The moon was full, and dozens of little upright shapes were casting long shadows

on the flagstones of the Sunk Garden. I saw the Duchess watching
out of the window, lights off. When I went into the drawing room
she was crouched over the fire reading a novel, the flames shivering
in the big diamond ring the Duke gave her and she never gave back.
'I hate them,' she said.

'Hate what?'

'The frogs. I hate the way they watch you.' I tried to point out
that in fact they were watching everyone, or more probably each
other. She would have none of it. I had to engage her in Scrabble to
divert her mind. 'Spring,' she said. 'So *vulgar*.'

I nodded. She put ZYGOTTIC on a triple word score, secure in the
knowledge that if I objected to the spelling she would be back on
the gin in a trice. The triple and the fifty-point bonus seemed to
soothe her, and she trudged off to bed in a state resembling smug-
ness. I took a last look out of the door.

The moon was low behind an orchard thickened with buds.
The daffodils were a pale splash under the crab apple trees. An owl
hooted from the ridge of the barn, and behind it was another noise,
if it was a noise. It was the sound of the lawn preparing to grow,
and the birds taking a few deep breaths, because they were going to
need all the breath they could get with the dawn. It was the sound
of the frogs getting ready to clear their throats, and the herbaceous
border about to bust forth, and the close-cut willows deciding to
pick themselves up, dust themselves down, and start all over again.
It was the silence that a wave makes when it has reared up and
hangs for one silent moment before it blasts forward with a long,
mighty roar. The silence, in fact, before the storm of spring.

Let it rage, we say, so we can surf on it, and never mind what the
readers of the *Tatler* think about the international situation. Even
the Duchess agrees.

Serendipitousness

DURING THE SECOND WEEK of May I looked out of the window and saw the Duchess wading across the croquet lawn with an expression of settled misery on her noble mush. She squelched into the morning room and cast herself on a Sheraton sofa. 'I can't take much more of this,' she said, her eye straying towards the door of the cupboard in which she keeps her emergency supplies.

You could see her point. Beyond the rain-dripped windows the gardens of the Hope stretched dismally away into the downpour. The borders were lush and green, studded with the shattered wrecks of peonies. The choisya, usually brilliant as a spring bride, looked like a spring bride who had been hauled by the hair through a lambing shed. The yews stood with their feet in the water, contemplating their reflections with the gloomy conviction that even if they lived for five thousand years, the whole of life would still be six to five against. From the depths of the house came the despairing howls of a rogue grandchild.

'It is supposed,' said the Duchess, 'to be summer.' As I have already observed, she had a point. But the way she said it, the born-to-rule, I-will-not-tolerate-this-stuffishness of her, was extremely annoying. And it is a known thing that in a house in the downpour in the Welsh Marches, the first flicker of irritation must be rigorously suppressed, lest it flare into a full-blown row, which can all too easily lead to acts of random cheating at Scrabble and thence to rehab, murder and cannibalism.

'There, there,' I said, soothingly. 'If summer has not come to us, we must go to summer.' And off we went to Sri Lanka.

In case you have not been there, this is an island where more or less perpetual summer obtains as long as there is no monsoon in place, which at that moment there wasn't. We got off an aeroplane and decompressed at the Galle Face Hotel in Colombo, an establishment whose acres of teak floors and unquestioning admiration for the cosmonaut Yuri Gagarin instantly endeared it to the Duchess.

Having acclimatised and engaged a driver, we then set off for the hills.

There are some pretty dreadful bits of Sri Lanka, which (as in many other spots on the face of the earth) include most of the places whose names are familiar in the West. But the Duchess has rightly pointed out that this is a garden essay, in which folk-dancing and Czech package tourists have no place. I shall therefore confine myself to discussing the vegetation, unless of course I get distracted.

The plains are with a few exceptions devoted to coconut trees and oil palms. Inland, matters improve. Hard alongside the ghastly metropolis of Kandy are the Peradeniya Botanic Gardens, which combine splendid plantings with some endearingly bizarre touches. On the practical end of things, they have a comprehensive palm grove, a garden devoted to indigenous herbs and dye plants, and an interesting fan of different types of tropical lawn plants, on at least two of which a cricket ball would bounce true. Supremely wonky Cook's pines shoot skywards from broad green meadows. Huge blue-green bamboos swarm down to a river that looks as it if ought to hold salmon. The principal avenue marches down to a sort of pedestrian roundabout, near which are trees planted by Yuri Gagarin (again), the Emperor of Japan (in very poor health) and Czar Nicholas II of Russia, which looks as if it had a severe shock to its system in about 1917.

At this point the visitor becomes aware of a high shrieking, and detects a curious smell, half fox, half compost heap. This emanates from the enormous flock of fruit bats that have their homes in the groves beyond the roundabout. We proceeded among vast forest trees, in each alcove of whose buttressed roots a courting couple lay writhing faintly. At the bottom of the garden a Regimental Sergeant-Major of a man in a khaki uniform with a sweeping moustache appointed himself our health and safety escort over an elegant Victorian suspension bridge, then extorted a tip in a high, wheedling voice that left the Duchess wishing (she said) to kick him.

Her mood had slipped, alas. The botanic garden pleased her, as it would please anyone of refined sensibility. But so far she had encountered nothing but tourism, and while she is as convinced a tourist as you are likely to meet in a long year's travel, she hates being called one. It was therefore with a nameless dread that I steered her into the next phase of the epic, viz. the train from Peradeniya to Ella.

Our staff had booked us seats in the observation car attached to the rear of the train. Observation is good, unmoderated by any luxuries like glass. The track ascends steeply into jungle, and the student of epiphytes will find much to admire. After two or three hours, the track ran along a dizzy arête with a mountain range stretching away on either side. Villages of white houses lay sprawled over the peaks, and below them the red earth had been neatly cut into terraces of the finest tilth, on which the local population, warmly dressed against the altitude, were weeding. The terraces bore post-Imperial runner beans, French and broad beans, carrots, beetroot, onions, shallots, leeks and lettuces, alongside the more exotic staples of bindi and chilli, which give the country's cooking its fiery deliciousness.

The Duchess gave a sigh audible even above the screech of wheels on track. '*Our* vegetables,' she said, and to my intense relief she actually smiled.

We descended towards Ella through hills furred with tea plantations, and rented a bungalow on a hillside. Women moved past, picking at high speed, exactly as on the PG Tips packet. It was news to the Duchess that tea is a form of camellia, and exists in a state of perpetual torment, its growing tips plucked out before they can mature. The hillsides where they grow are hottish, studded with *shivalingams* wrapped in tinsel scarves, and emanate a faint, bracing air. Occasionally a tea bush has been allowed to flower. Its scent is heavy, in the jasmine order of things. As we stood on a mountain spur looking south across the coastal plain to the distant Indian Ocean, the Duchess observed that a whole hillside of tea flowers would smell like a tart's boudoir. To express her gratitude at the non-occurrence of this state of affairs she gave one of the Tamil pluckers a dazzling smile. The Tamil ran for her life. It began to rain. We headed downhill.

The heat was pretty intense at sea level, and the Duchess expressed her intention to spend some time on her back examining the crown of a particular palm tree that spread its shadow over a patch of white and lonely beach. We recuperated in a compound of huts and strelitzias and mango trees, waiting for the mountain leech-bites to heal up and developing the aesthetic sense like hey-my-nanny. Finally, we were ready, and made a pilgrimage to Geoffrey Bawa's garden at Lunaganga, where a reverent youth conducted us on a tour. I shall make only two observations about this garden. One is that by the side of a lotus pool in the form of twin butterfly wings, a medium-sized crocodile was basking, possibly in a state of digestion. The other is that Lunaganga contains a fine specimen of the Hijacked Vista, as popularised by Repton, in which the designer points the principal avenue at a feature – in this case a *dagoba*, or Buddhist spire-and-dome combo – that does not belong to him, but that he likes the look of. In order to make the HV more agreeable, Bawa removed the top of an intervening hill.

The Duchess thoroughly approved of all this, and would talk of nothing else on the aeroplane home. One nodded, and smiled, and hoped she would forget all about it. But as I write this in the green shade of the pleached lime with the sun striking pearly through the glass of pastis at my elbow, I have a nasty feeling that she is over on the other side of the valley among the neighbours' chicken sheds, theodolite and callipers in hand, plotting architectural mayhem. One more pastis, and I shall start to prepare my defence.

Serpents of the Marches

THE EQUINOX HAS COME AND GONE, and it looks as if autumn is icumen in, lhude sing yarboo. Not as lhude as usual, though. At least the early sunsets will draw a veil of darkness over one of the most horticulturally disastrous seasons since the Plagues of Egypt. One of the many tedious things about this is that everyone you meet is putting up a strong beef about the weather situation. So I suppose it is my duty to strike the positive note. First, though, there are things that need getting out of the way.

One melancholy evening in the downpour that passed for summer, an odd strangled noise emanated from the general direction of the sofa. In the livid glare of a lightning flash I perceived that it was being produced by the Duchess, frozen by the sudden illumination into an attitude indicative of struggle. Furthermore it seemed to me that the heady glow of her necklace of Agra rubies – a gift from some Maharajah or other, and a thoughtless one, as it is well known that rubies aggravate the aggressive side of the female nature, which in the case of the Duchess amounts to pouring petrol on an already raging fire – was dulled by an odd serpentine ligature that seemed to have become entangled in the necklace. Given the mugginess of the evening I could not be bothered to get up. After some consideration I decided it was probably a snake.

Reaching for my copy of Gould's *Serpents of the Marches*, I began to leaf through. The ligature seemed too long for a *krait*, and too slim for a puff adder. Perhaps, I thought gloomily, it is one of the non-venomous types which from time to time raise then dash the hopes of loved ones with expectations. But Gould is a fascinating book, with plates of the highest quality, and naturally I became distracted. I was examining the section on Pit Vipers when a hideous gargling rang in the coffering. 'The speckled band!', croaked the Duchess. Not, of course, original; but it seemed to indicate a level of distress that I could not in all conscience ignore, particularly if she survived and had a chance to talk to the police. So I seized the poker and leaped forward. And discovered, as I tore with heroic fingers at the thing among the rubies, that it was not a snake at all, but a length of bindweed.

That has been the way of it this year. The plants we have divided, massaged and fed like celebrities at a health farm sat during the early summer in patches of brown earth and glowered, achieving nothing in the way of growth or inflorescence. The dustbins filled with rain, once, twice, three times. No growth took place, except on the part of the weeds. And weeding was hard. For one thing, whenever the downpour resumed it was necessary to get off the ground before it began to look like Passchendaele. More importantly, it is impossible to keep a personal music machine dry under the monsoon. The Duchess claims to have learned her weeding to the strains of the band of the Brigade of Guards, though I doubt this. I myself started in glum silence and escaped to talking books. There is nothing like a good Mafia thriller, perhaps *The Winter of Frankie Machine*, to get you extirpating docks. Revel in the ghastly behaviour of Mrs Proudie as you charge through head-high groundsel among the Indian corn, and laugh along with Gussie Fink-Nottle at the Market Snodsbury Grammar School prize-giving as you remove fat hen from the potato bed. Under these circs, weeding becomes more of a joy than a chore. Fill your personal stereo with rain, though, and you are cast back on your own resources, already stretched to cracking point. Reader, we gave up.

So the bindweed has taken over the parts that the nettles have not already colonised, and the only fruit and flowers we have in this season of mists and yellow fruitlessness are coming out of the greenhouse. I can tell that the Duchess feels it keenly, even when she is not being half-strangled by rogue tendrils creeping in at the window. Recent inspections of the gin bottle have revealed that the layer of dust is more or less intact; but there are the marks of fingers, as if she has had it out of the cupboard, revolved it in hand and mind, and put it back again. It is apparent that a scheme is needed before she is zigzagging down the High Street singing sea shanties.

And I think we have got one.

It involves water, of which, as I have already pointed out, there seems to be plenty around. The Hope, as I have also pointed out, is one of Britain's premier hilltop swamps. We are therefore considering building a berm or earth wall round most of it, and allowing the rainfall to convert it into a gigantic pond, which will form the basis for a new garden. We will build crannogs, on which there will be island beds in the purest sense. But this will not be a normal watery garden, with a few bright willows and dogwoods and the obligatory drifts of arriviste kingcups. Oh, no. For by then we will have bought a new personal stereo, and we will be out there weeding in a chartered Cardiff Bay dredger. Once the task is finished, channels will weave through great fields of zantedeschias in colours between blood-red and night-black. Parts of the lake will be shallow enough to grow sheets of *arc-en-ciel* and other beautiful water lilies. Other parts will be bottomlessly deep, and into one of these we will throw the personal stereo, and take a recruiting trip to Xochimilco in the suburbs of Mexico City.

In case you have not already been there, Xochimilco is the last remnant of the floating gardens whose vegetables fed the Aztecs before the arrival of the Conquistadors. Canals thread nurseries and gardens of vegetables and flowers, and on the canals are boats. Some of the boats carry members of the public taking their ease. Others carry orchestras – mariachi bands, with the big hats and the plaintive trumpets, and norteño bands, with squeeze-boxes and plangent guitars, and men in white pyjamas from the distant jungles of Chiapas playing things made out of tortoises. As soon as your boat noses into the stream, two orchestra boats appear from nowhere and clamp themselves one to each side. You dismiss the one you like least, which is instantly replaced by another, until by a process of elimination you arrive at your favourite. You are then serenaded, while from time to time men with buckets of ice bring you bottles of beer and tequila.

We shall be adapting this process to suit the calmer British temperament. We will bring home our favourite mariachi, true. But some of our punts will carry string quartets, while others will carry folk singers to regale us with songs about the herring as we drift past the knobbly knees of the swamp cypresses. There may even be a fisher hermit mending his gear before a netshed *orné*. We are still arguing about the resident philosopher. The Duchess wants an Epicurean, and I want a Stoic. The odds are that we will end up with neither. But with all those water lilies we might get a real anaconda in at the drawing room window. Much better than bindweed.

It is only teatime, but it is already dark. Turn on the lights and open the wine. There are plans to draw.

Shanties

BLOW, YE WINDS, and crack your cheeks. Also the enamel on our teeth, the way things are going. One day everyone is sitting in an arctic blast, and the next, warm fug is screaming in from the Atlantic. Frankly we do not know what to think, so the Duchess has decided that we will concentrate on singing instead.

It has been a good year for singing. During the summer monsoon everyone became unused to the idea of wandering around outdoors and gathered round the baby grand with a spot of sheet music. We watched out of the windows as we sang *Only God Can Make a Tree*, while the trees and the weeds grew, and the flowers didn't. Eventually we went abroad, donned snorkels, and floated, bubbling tunefully, over gardens of polychrome seaweed that somehow felt drier than the stodgy Welsh Marches.

The vegetable harvest was odd, and caused a brief silence. Sun-dependent stuff unsurprisingly showed signs of *weltschmerz* — sweet-corn white and unappetizing as baby axolotls, and artichokes merely going through the motions. Some things did not happen at all, notably the Arran Pilots and some of the broad beans. Cabbages, however, grew gigantic, as did French beans. In the polytunnels the tomatoes succumbed to blight, while the chilli peppers multiplied amazingly. We will not speak of the fruit, hard or soft, top or bottom, because there was none to speak of, let alone sing about.

The proceeds of autumn amounted to some quince jelly, a spot of crab apple ditto, and several jars of pickled chillies so ferocious that they are best approached with a revolver and a chair. We have poured dry sherry on top of other chillies, and found that song returned in the form of the following shanty, composed by the Duchess specially for the occasion:

I was marinating Sherry Chilli Peppers
When my sherry got swiped by a bunch of lepers
Crying, 'Drink that chilli sherry! It will make us whole!'
Tried to stop those lepers running off with my peppers

(Lepers can be really obstreperous)
[shouts]
'Leave that sherry right there in that bowl!'

Now the jars are sealed, and the pickled substances are emitting
a faint radioactive glow in the bottom left-hand cupboard in the
back larder; and we are faced with the problem of what to do next.
We were abroad so much this year that as I have implied, the
beds took on a hostile runaway air. In autumn we divided herbaceous clumps and lined out the results to use as swaps with our
friends and neighbours, humming as we dug. We also swathed certain sensitive bamboos in horticultural fleece, to stop them getting
razed to the ground again. This gave rise to another shanty – one
that might perhaps have been written by Ernest 'Chinese' Wilson
in the Min valley just before the First World War:

> *Listen to the breezes in the sinarundinaria*
> *Hearken to the zephyrs in the new bamboo!*
> *There will be rejoicing in a minor London area*
> *When a specimen arrives at Kew*
> *Oo hoo*
> *When a specimen arrives at Kew.*

This, I have to confess, is my own composition. The Duchess,
deeply suspicious as always of anything that was not her idea in
the first place, pointed out that *Sinarundinaria murielae*, named by
Wilson for his daughter, is now known as *Fargesia murielae*, which
mucks up the rhyme. There was a bit of a row about this, and the
Duchess stumped off to the kitchen garden, where I heard the clash
of her fork-tines against loose stones and her harsh but noble voice
creaking out the following *sloka*:

> *Dig Dig Dig*
> *Damn you*
> *Dig Dig Dig.*

Having purified her soul with effort, she came indoors to

complain about the cold, and I was forced to admit that she had a point. We are not burning any oil because of the trouble in the Gulf and at the bank. We were therefore cast back on our own resources – a thorny place, but one stimulating to horticultural initiative. And sure enough, there was a breakthrough.

Twenty-odd years ago, we planted several thousand trees. Most of them were the regional mixture of oak and ash, with (thanks to the hallucinations of the Forestry Commission representative of the time, who may have been confused as to the exact whereabouts of the Scottish border) a sprinkling of birch and rowan. The day after the *sinarundinaria* contretemps I was leaning on a fork in the border, resting the eye on a clump of willows into which a Greater spotted woodpecker had just blundered, when I saw something rusty poking out of the top. Abandoning the fork – any excuse, really – I marched into the spinney. And was surprised and delighted to find, lurking among the plebeian butts of the willows, a black sycamore, a well-grown Scots pine, and best of all a dawn redwood, whose needles had turned their autumn russet and were about to decade. I had known perfectly well it was there, of course; it was merely that it had slipped my mind.

Anyway. Out came the instruments of destruction, and down came the willows. The chainsaw is a useful accompaniment to a song about the rediscovery of lost trees, producing at high revs a howl of agony and at low revs a drone conducive to folk song. This we used as a background for a version of *John Riley*, in which a maiden, whose eponymous fiancé has for some years been missing, presumed drowned, meets a stranger by the strand, discovers that he is indeed her own long lost John Riley, and lives happily ever after. The chainsaw version of the song goes:

> *I will get a*
> *Chain saw to annoy these*
> *Willows and reveal meta*
> *sequoia glyptostroboides.*

There are hundreds more verses.

Anyway. We cut the willows into cordwood and stacked them for an eighteen-month dryout, after which they burn better than you would think. And where they had stood there remained a really charming grove of trees, trunks self-pruned thanks to the nurse trees, backed by a hawthorn hedge which we have trimmed into a fine green wall. Soon we will plant some rhododendrons at their bases. The whole experience has been most satisfactory.

> The weather may be cold
> The weather may be hot
> But a spinney is a lovesome thing, God wot.
> The sun may shine
> And the wind may blow
> A rhododendron is a lovesome thing, (or may be so).

There is more, but you do not need to hear it. Also satisfactory has been the behaviour of a row of holly 'Silver King', interspersed with the dullish 'J. C. van Tol' as a pollinator, which the Duchess insisted we plant some years ago as a hedge against recession. Recession or not, it is certainly a hedge nowadays, and pretty densely covered in red berries. We will be taking a good trailerful of it, mixed with mistletoe from the orchard, to the Christmas decorations auction in Tenbury in order to finance an order of festive stimulants. As we trundle down the wintry lanes we will be singing:

> O the hollying and mistletoeing
> When the auction hammer biffs
> Is like the starter's pistol going
> On dark red wine and white snow drifts.

Though of course the Duchess prefers gin, which she is not allowed, and we could not think of a rhyme for 'elderflower cordial' except 'smelter tower ordeal,' which lacks that ring.

So before you know it, earth will be standing hard as iron, water like a stone, and we will be scratching around for salad leaves in the polytunnel and admiring the frost-patterns on the eupatorium skeletons. If, that is, we go out at all. For there is a fire inside, and a lot of stuff to read. Until the moment when all starts turning green again, and we can sing

> *Hal an tow*
> *Jolly rumbelow*
> *We were up*
> *Long before the day o*
> *To welcome in the morning*
> *To welcome in the may o*
> *For summer is a-coming in*
> *And winter's gone away o.*

Bring it on.

Full Steam Ahead

A LONG AND LANDLOCKED WINTER has slabbered to an end. The covers are off the kitchen garden, where the worms have selflessly transported tons of muck into the depths. In the poly-tunnels the rows of intensely fashionable microgreens are about to turn into the less fashionable but infinitely more edible lettuces. Some of the larger puddles are receding, and a smell of deep green promise wells from the air.

Not that this makes any difference to the Duchess. For some months now she has been locked in to her turret, and we toilers in the garden have become suspicious to the point where we have taken to making up excuses to pass under her windows. It is on the way between (for instance) the herbaceous border and the fig trees; so there are sudden pauses in the middle of weeding to go and break off the frosted proto-figs. During these transitions shoelaces frequently need to be tied at the tower's foot, and an ear bent for the clank of gin bottle on glass, and an eye cast hither and yon for fresh Capstan Full Strength butts on the ground. Though if there were any butts, they would long ago have been used as the founda-tion of anti-greenfly potions. (Did you know, by the way, that some Australian birds have taken to making their nests out of filter tip fag ends? One of the banes of small-bird life is their attractiveness to mites and other insects, and the nicotine in the fag ends apparently ensures a lack of crawlers in the home environment. When I told the Duchess this she told me not to be disgusting and boring at the same time. She is really not in a healthy frame of mind, interested in the changing seasons and the passing scene. A psychiatrist would describe her as 'up herself'. Though the general view of the house-hold is that she has got post-traumatic stress disorder, based on actually being nice to someone at a drinks party some time around Christmas. Whether or not this is true, she tends to wake up in the middle of the night screaming 'Canapés! Damn all canapés', and needs soothing with massive draughts of chloral hydrate, of which we discovered a cask in the cellar the other week.)

But this is by the by, which is of course the reason it appears in brackets. We have, as it happens, been engaged in some largish operations during the closing days of winter. These have featured the construction of a couple of arbours, close inspection of the woods and various standard *Fraxinus ornus* for signs of dieback, and the replacement of the Giant Egg with the plywood silhouette of a nude, loosely based on the statuettes awarded at the Oscars. I am further preoccupied with modifying a small yacht into a floating library-cum-coldframe, for a trip I am making up the coast of Scotland. This is an interesting project, but the Duchess finds it, like the other stuff, tedious. And as all the world knows, a Duchess bored is a Duchess teetering on the brink of a vast lagoon of gin.

Then just as the daffodils were going over the telephone rang, and there on the other end was Nick Walker. Nick is the Captain of *Vic 32*, the only Clyde puffer still steaming up and down the west coast of Scotland. Once, the puffers carried coal, red herrings, passengers and any other cargoes they could find between the towns of this wild and beauteous area, separated by hundreds of miles of road but short distances by sea. Their adventures are chronicled in Neil Munro's very funny Para Handy stories – indeed, *Vic 32* played Para Handy's ship, the *Vital Spark*, in a recent television adaptation.

Nick and a corps of volunteers have turned her into a comfortable, if not actually luxurious, midget cruise ship. It is not generally known that steamships are almost silent. So passengers on *Vic 32* sit in the breeze and even the sun, hearing the panicky cries of the oystercatchers along the shore and the bubbling yodel of great northern divers in season . . .

Any minute now someone is going to say, wait a minute, this is a gardening essay, not a PR puff for seagoing steam freaks. Patience. There is horticulture in store. Here it comes.

The horticultural note is first struck by the tomato plants growing in *Vic 32*'s wheelhouse, warmed by the heat rising from the engine and brightened by the sun streaming in through the big plate-glass windows. It continues with the general flora of this part of Scotland, which is a kind of motorway pile-up of the seasons – primroses flowering at the same time as bluebells flowering at the same time as orchids flowering at the same time as foxgloves.

But the highest type of horticulture is visible in *Vic 32*'s itinerary, which in the late spring takes in some of that fine family of gardens, warmed by the Gulf Stream, in which plants more closely associated with Australia than Caledonia survive and thrive. The first time I ever saw Ardmaddy was after a cold, wet and frightening voyage south in a very small sailing boat from the waters north of Ardnamurchan, where trees are a rarity and the mountains slink through the clouds like enormous surly animals. Ardmaddy sits behind the shore warm and elegant, with a tower that owes more to the round towers of Ireland than the Franco-Germanic fantasies of the Scots baronial. The round towers were built, it was said, to protect the culture of Irish Christianity from the Vikings. The tower at Ardmaddy seems to exercise a similarly protective effect on the botanical treasures at its foot.

Here and at Arduaine, a few miles away by water, it is a help to like rhododendrons – particularly in June, when *Vic 32* makes her most horticultural voyages. But these are not sheets of grimly kaleidoscopic Home Counties hybrids. Species abound, and so do scented versions unknown by the shores of Virginia Water. The effect is more Bhutan than Basingstoke, but a Bhutan at the foot of whose glens the Sea of the Hebrides gleams dully, rolling, if you are lucky, with dolphins and whales.

A tedious distance away by road, but a hop and a skip by puffer, is An Cala, somewhat tamer than the two above, but kept temperate by the same Gulf Stream waters as its neighbours. Here, the echiums are as tall as (if slightly later than) the ones on Tresco, and there is a sort of post-Arts-and-Crafts matiness that can make you forget you are in Scotland at all.

This is the only worry I have about taking the Duchess on *Vic 32*. She does not really do matey, and her vision of Scotland has been largely formed in Accident and Emergency clinics following adventures at Caledonian Balls and grouse drives. In those days her idea of breakfast north of the border was to stump up and down the dining room with a bowl of porridge in one hand and a large gin in the other, Capstan Full Strength clipped between her fingers, which nicotine had tanned to the colour of the bark of an *Acer griseum*. But that was then, and this is now. Perhaps she will behave.

So I have pushed a bit of paper bearing the magic words www. savethepuffer.co.uk under her door. She will no doubt wish to travel on the *Hebridean Princess*, and so would we all, including the Queen, who uses the ship as a Royal Yacht since that unpleasant Mr Blair spitefully confiscated *Britannia*. But the puffer, being smaller, gets closer to the action.

Talking about which, the year is rolling on. It is time to mark the daffodils for moving, plant some more potatoes, cut back the buddleias, and perhaps put a couple of chairs within range of the big stone table. Scotland will not be fit for habitation for a month or two yet. Meanwhile spring is rolling like a green tide up the hills of the Marches, and we will have to work like demons to keep our heads above it, and if the Duchess wishes to sulk, that is her business, not ours.

But here she comes, out of the tower door, dressed in an orange Tarmac boiler suit and some of her second-best diamonds. She pulls a hoe from the toolshed and makes a couple of dummy swings, like a golfer at the tee. Clearly she means business. Thank goodness for that.

Lenin on Lawn Care

I KNOW, I KNOW. I am supposed to be writing about summer in the garden at the Hope. But this year the detail has frankly escaped me. The roses are up and about, particularly the ever-reliable 'John Transom' clustering round and indeed in at the studio window. The stocks are wafting scent hither and yon, the poppies are blowing, and the sedums and sempervivums are motivating over their wall like little Martian armies. But my view of the place is rather more remote than that of, say, a slug or an American satellite. As usual this is down to the Duchess.

It started in the spring. I do not know if you can cast your mind back that far, or indeed if you have the moral strength. It was as if Ma Nature went off on holiday somewhere nice and warm, and failed to shut the freezer door before she left. This had a depressing effect on the nation as a whole and the Duchess in particular. It came to a head one morning when we were staring glumly out of the breakfast room window. A thin sun was glancing off the pond in the sunk garden. The ice was rubbly with frozen frogspawn. The sedge was withered and no birds sang. 'Blow this,' said the Duchess (except 'blow' was not the word she used) 'for a lark.'

I said, amusingly I thought, that what with the winter and now this I could not remember what a lark looked like. She gave me the cold stare. I asked her to stop looking at me as if she was Meyer Lansky eying a punter who had failed to come up with the vig, and to make the best of a bad situation.

The ceiling swam with bloody lights from the rubies on her fingers as she tore her napkin into confetti. 'The pathetic jokes I do not mind,' she said. 'It is taking poor Meyer's name in vain that I will not tolerate. He was kind to me as a child.'

As you probably know, the Duchess has in her time been remarkably keen on Plymouth gin and Capstan Full Strength cigarettes, and I saw her eyes stray towards the heavily-fortified cupboard in which the stimulants are nowadays placed for safe keeping. If we were to avoid relapse, followed by sea shanties, self-reproach and rehab, swift action was absolutely necessary. 'So what will you tolerate?' I said, all emollient.

'I haven't seen Meyer for ages,' she said.

Now I happen to know that Meyer Lansky, besides having been the Mafia kingpin of pre-revolutionary Cuba, has been dead since 1983. I did not however wish to mention either of those things, as the Duchess is one of those strong-minded people who infinitely prefers finding out to being told. So I said, 'Why don't we go to Cuba?' Thinking, of course, that once I had her somewhere warm and bright, I could get her on to horticulture, and her megrims would melt away.

So away we flew, and a nice man called Carlos took us through customs, who seemed to be cousins of his, and to a pleasing hotel built round a courtyard with some fat bamboos and a traveller's palm planted in its middle. The Duchess was looking brighter already, puffing at a large cigar and going into unnecessary detail about the provenance of some rather ordinary pelargoniums tumbling down the pillars. Next day we visited the municipal parks of Havana, which are charming indeed, though none too floral. There are curious choices of garden statuary here and there, in the shape of American aeroplanes that seem to have met with nasty accidents, and brutalist concrete *stelae* bearing inspiring slogans. (Comrades! It is through horticulture and good attitude that we will conquer!)

The Duchess was visibly overexcited now. She marched across the grass, shoved a soldier brusquely to one side, and surged into what seemed to be a museum. Here she scowled at a glass case containing the bloody gardening pyjamas of an insurgent shot while hoeing, muttered her way through the revolutionary campaigns of the 1950s, and came to rest in front of a photograph of Fidel Castro and Che Guevara playing clock golf. Her *voce* was now well above *sotto*, and thickset attendants were closing in. 'Look at that!' she said, indicating the clock golf pitch with a shaking finger. 'Bloody communists!'

It is true that the turf was strewn with what looked like dandelions. But there had just been a revolution, and in the writings of Lenin even the most diligent groundsman finds very little advice about lawn care. What the Duchess will never understand is that what Lenin leaves undiscussed is *de facto* condemned by his adherents as bourgeois, i.e. roughly as desirable as greenfly at Wisley. (Though if you called her *bourgeoise*, this scion of Crusaders and Palace courtesans would certainly set the dogs on you.) As she started screaming about dandelions in Spanish I managed with some difficulty to drag her away and place her in an old pink Cadillac. In this we thundered out of Havana and into the hinterland.

As all the world knows the Cubans are not on the best of terms with the Americans, who still seem to hold it against them that they tried to start the Third World War in 1962. There is nothing like your American government for harbouring a grudge, particularly when egged on by the many right-wing Cubans who live in Florida, notoriously a swing state in Presidential elections. And there is nothing like an American government grudge, backed up by a trade embargo, for developing self-reliance in a fertile tropical island. Ornamental gardening as such is not much rated as a pursuit for Cuban grown-ups. But the Botanic Garden of Cienfuegos, founded in pre-Revolutionary days to develop bigger and better varieties of sugar cane, is splendid by any criteria. Its collection is now large and interesting. In the 1950s it was the base for the Harvard Tropical Botany course. There is not much Ivy League about it nowadays, but the Duchess was favourably impressed by its enormously long avenue of Royal palms (*Roystonea dunlapiana*) and its gigantic clumps of bamboo overhanging a river in which gardeners fish lackadaisically for dead leaves. There is also a rockery, which looks like a set for one of the less popular episodes of *Star Trek*. But (as the Duchess pointed out, giving proof of a practically supernatural mellowing) the acacia collection is delightful, and as for the rockery, into each life a little rain must fall.

No rain falls on the roof terraces of Trinidad, though. This is a charming town set among green mountains. At street level it is all cobbles and ancient patios and guitar music. At roof level, the treescape mixes with the tilescape and gives way to a distant seascape. Some of the trees are ceibas, otherwise known as kapok, remarkable vegetables locally rumoured to stump very slowly across the landscape in the night, doing good. Their seedpods produce a cotton-wool-like fibre used to stuff lifejackets and pillows. Sleepers on *ceiba* pillows are guaranteed excellent dreams, which anchor Cubans to their island even when they are far away.

One evening we were watching the sun set over the sea and listening to the voices and the guitars ringing in the stone streets when the Duchess said, 'That's enough abroad.'

I shushed her, for I was listening to a peculiarly effective phrase on a well-twanged *tres*. She got up and went indoors, and from the sound of breaking glass I deduced that she had started packing. And six weeks later, here we are back at the Hope. The frosts have gone, and the rains have come. Apparently spring has shot by. The yew hedges are fuzzed with golden shoots, and the borders are a discreet kaleidoscope. The table is up under the lime, and lunch is on it, except for the salad, which the Duchess, with a calmness we had all thought foreign to her nature, is picking in the kitchen garden. I have just walked out to the table across a lawn that has been colonised by dandelions, dammit. I am now sitting down, taking some notes. The sun between the lime leaves is leaving a scattering of little gold medals across the tablecloth, except where the rays are finding their way through my glass of Château de Sours, where the medals are a good fresh pink. I will drink to the people, music and vegetation of Cuba, to clock golf as the pinnacle of the socialist dream, and confusion to Lenin and his dandelions. *¡Salud!*

Canada Ho!

IT IS THAT TIME OF YEAR AGAIN. The rosé wine of summer has turned mawkish on the palate, and thicker, redder vintages are being hauled up from the cellar. The mellow fruitfulness has been terrific, and many hundredweight of apples have been wrapped in paper and laid in cool, airy sheds, ready for weekly survey and excavation in the long cold months. In a fortified manor house down the road squaddies from the local army camp are turning an ancient cider press, stimulated by last year's brew, until they stumble singing hoarsely into the first frosts. So mighty has the apple harvest been, indeed, that the proprietor has decided to exceed his Customs quota by several thousand gallons, burying the surplus in cylindrical drums among the trees so that on warmish days the casual walker is astounded by what appear to be volcanic fumaroles bursting from the sward.

In spite of all this, the Duchess has been professing herself discontented with the normal run of the seasons. Ignoring the fact that during the sodden summer of 2012 she did nothing but make remarks about it being all right for people with webbed feet, she has spent most of 2013 lurking about the garden in what pools of shadow she has been able to find, beefing about the heat. As I set out to lift onions one morning her voice hissed like a razor from an inky notch in the Stepped Hedge. 'Get me,' she said, in a weird gasping voice, 'out of here'.

Plucking a rheum leaf as a swift parasol, I shepherded her back to the house. She was babbling about coolth, whatever that is. I put her in a low medieval room, and she instantly started to tear books down from the shelf. Having hung around long enough to make sure that no Plymouth gin and Capstan Full Strength were hidden in the shelves, I left, and started in on the groundsel, 2013's Weed of the Year. Eventually the lunch gong sounded, and in we trooped. The Duchess was already there. In a ray of sun that slanted from the clerestory windows and through her mineral water lay a book: Grenfell's *Labrador*. 'That,' said the Duchess, 'is where we must go.'

At this point I experienced a pronounced sinking of the heart. Coolth is all very well, but there is little to be said for icebergs, particularly when they are wallowing in a sea lashed to grey slate by a thick driving rain. Furthermore, the vegetation of Labrador is limited to pine trees and some of the kind of Arctic willows grown by trainspotter-style enthusiasts on the smaller rockery. Once again, the Duchess was demonstrating her propensity for extremes.

I prepared to mine the seams of tact which must be exploited to cool her ardour, rather as asbestos lagging surrounds a red-hot boiler. The first thing to do was to agree. 'Quite so,' I said. 'A fascinating, nay inspired, choice. Though perhaps a little far north for personal comfort, and rather wet. What,' I said, in the spirit of compromise, 'about Atlanta, Georgia?'

'Yellowknife,' she said, quick as a flash.

'The Great Smoky Mountains of North Carolina.'

'Yellowknife,' she said again, and I knew from bitter experience that Horticultural Destination Poker had reached a critical point. 'Quebec,' I said.

'James Bay,' she said, naming a point in the far north.

'The South Shore of the St Lawrence,' I said.

She sulked, but I had the cards, and she comes from a long line of sporting if incompetent gamblers. So she agreed, and later that week the shadow of our Airbus was flicking over rocks and trees and the broad muddy channel of the Seaway.

One of the Duchess's uncles was Governor-General in the days when Governors-General still ate their breakfasts wearing cocked hats with ostrich plumes. His orchid house had once been the toast of Ottawa, and the Duchess claimed she longed to see it. Alas, our visit was a failure. Where once phalaenopsis had sweltered in its stove among the boreal snows, a branch of Tim Horton's, purveyor of soggy donuts, lowered at an expressway. I sensed that the Duchess's mood was beginning to totter, and took her off to Montreal.

She frowned at the Botanic Gardens, which are famous for their topiary, much of which seems to have been designed by the *kitschmeister* Jeff Koons on a slow morning. So we took a taxi into the city for lunch. The horticultural decoration of the city centre was charming. Well-grown castor oil plants brimming with health sat

in carpets of maroon-leaved begonias. Elsewhere, more begonias
with enormous pale-green leaves flourished on vast billows of
busy-Lizzies. The effect was deeply psychedelic, and the Duchess
mentioned that it would probably have given Christopher Lloyd
a heart attack. But she seemed pacified, and the memory carried
her through to the next stage of our journey, out of the city and
on to the motorway that runs along the southern bank of the St
Lawrence. This is a landscape of such vastness and tedium that
it is impossible to contemplate it without feeling very sorry for
the first Europeans to set foot here, wearing porous clothes and
without insect repellent. Sympathy rapidly changed to irritation as
we contemplated the vast agricultural monocultures of the coastal
strip, interspersed with silos and the gigantic churches erected by
local Catholics to serve the tiny populations of the scattered towns.
Private gardens need defensible space – indeed, the word garden is
held by some to derive from OE *wardjan*, walled enclosure, which
the Duchess, born and bred in a castle, was quick to point out has
strong implications of defence and privacy.

The houses of the South Shore do not do this. They are plonked
down in boggy fields in small groups hemmed in by the forest pri-
meval but otherwise unfenced. South Shore horticulture means a
small lump of busy-Lizzies out the front, colour irregardless (as
they say round here) as long as it is bright. These patches sit in the
lawn before the parent house rather as the beginning of a migraine
vibrates in the sufferer's eye. At first it is hard to imagine that they
possess any aesthetic merit. But finally I managed to navigate myself round to the view that merit they do possess, and very much
in the *wardjan* sense.

I told the Duchess as much as we sat bathed in golden sunlight
on the stoop of a shack in a clearing deep in the woods. The evening
air had a definite edge to it. We had spent the afternoon as part of
a human chain, shifting the last five tons of the winter's firewood
– bone-dry maple, beautifully split – into the basement, where the
stove stood ready to burn the full twenty-five tons and spread their
heat up through the gaps in the floorboards to warm the house in
the -20° days to come. Down from the north the Fall was sweeping,
and the leaves of the woods were turning an astonishing gamut of

colours, gamboge through rust and tangerine to deepest crimson. It is a riot of colour in the best possible taste, spread over millions of acres. The migraine patches of impatiens in front of the houses gave this vastness (I observed to the Duchess) a human scale, and put things in proportion.

She looked at me coldly. 'What a lot of nonsense,' she said. 'They're ghastly, and you know it.' Her ruby necklace rattled as she shivered. 'It's cold.'

'Not as cold as Labrador,' I said.

So we came home, and found something of an Indian summer in progress. We went to Clovelly Court, where the garden has been restored to astonishing perfection, and gazed down borders full of the last of the dahlias, at the roll of the park and the rusty oak woods descending to the cliffs and the great blue sea shifting beyond. The air was full of the hum of late bees. 'East, west, home's best,' said the Duchess with a sigh.

If only she meant it.

Money for Old Rope

AUTUMN IS OVER. We have raked up the leaves. We have rolled the hedgehogs into safe places. We have stocked the bird table with niger seed for the goldfinches and suet for the rats. We have planted wallflowers on the Home Beach, and hidden the jungle chaos of the kitchen garden under grim black sheets of Mypex. We have brought in the hackings of Scotch pines liberated by the creation of the Caledonian Glade and flung them on the fire. We have . . .

Here I must pause, because the Duchess has just thrown the De Jaeger wholesale bulb catalogue at my head, and I have ducked, and the wine is running into the typewriter. The Duchess has become rather inflammable lately. It is a result of her being underemployed – not that she has ever done a hand's turn in her life; lately she has used any excuse, even wildly unlikely ones, to be edgy, edgy.

It started early in the year with the Grand National. She put her shirt on a 100–1 outsider which fell, as everyone except her knew it would, at the first fence. Moneymaking schemes followed thick and fast. First there was going to be a linen mill, supplied with fibres from a great hedge of phormiums that has been growing boring but unchecked in the South Stockade. She was deaf to all remarks that linen was made out of linum, not phormium, and that the name was a clue. We all had to go out and cut the leaves and tie them in bundles and fling them in the horse pond to rot, or ret, as she called it, though nobody else could tell the difference. A couple of weeks later the water lilies died and we had to call the vet to a mandarin duck which had taken an injudicious swig on a hot day. The Duchess caused the slimy remnants to be extracted, dried them on a sort of frame, and engaged a spinner and a weaver, who produced after much labour something that looked like a potato sack woven from pure mud. This the Duchess presented to Ermenegildo Zegna when he came to dinner. We found it next morning jammed into a crevice of the Triton Fountain, where the great designer had stuffed it before being driven off to his private jet.

This was discouraging, and for a moment the Duchess's eyes strayed towards the cupboard, now covered with a thick layer of dust, where the Plymouth gin and Capstan Full Strength are stored to show that she can handle them any time, but chooses not to. Then to everyone's relief her eye skidded away and lighted on the Yellow Book. She instantly went to her desk, pulled out the cream laid sheets festooned with strawberry leaves, and started writing. The following day she took the letters to the Post Office in a wheelbarrow and informed me that the garden would henceforward be open to the public on Tuesdays and Thursdays by appointment. It was a surprise to me that in a democracy like ours, people would flock to hear an aristocratic rehab veteran with a rasping voice and gigantic emeralds banging on about a garden which, it being winter, had many of the characteristics of a blasted heath. But in the coaches came, one after another, and out poured the multitudes.

The Duchess relieved the drivers of bundles of large coarse notes, and conducted the tours herself. I kept as far away as possible and made like a hired hand. It was however hard to avoid occasional glimpses of the seekers after horticultural truth. At the beginning, the Duchess was to be seen leading gangs of them past the Assymetric Yews, pointing out significant roses, cursing all lavateras ('filthy hairy little khaki brutes'), and taking the sting out of her remarks with the dazzling smile. As the year rolled on she became sullen, perhaps through exhaustion, and once I had to dissuade her from forcing a Midlands Women's Institute chairperson who had asked a silly question ('What is that thing up there?') to climb a tree to find out the answer ('Someone's hat.')

It all came to a head one difficult day in late November. I had been removing bindweed from the asparagus bed with a surgeon's care, and had paused for a rapid lunch when I heard a sound like a gunshot. This was followed a low growling, as of a bucko mate instructing a ship's crew to make preparations for an imminent hurricane. It was proceeding from the kitchen garden, and thither I made my way with a lump of cheese in my hand and fear in my heart.

The sight that met my eyes was a sobering one. There in the potato bed was a busload of ladies of a certain age wearing print dresses and strung out in a ragged line. They were moving slowly across the brown and fertile earth, from which the potatoes had been lifted a month or so previously. Their poor fingers were tunnelling in the soil. And behind them, revolver in one hand and hunting crop in the other, strode the Duchess, restless as a tiger. 'Grovel!' she cried. 'Grovel and grope, ye daughters of Belial, and if there be a single adventitious potato plant or mutcher as we call them round these parts, I shall hunt you down with security operatives and have the hides off your miserable backs.'

'Aye, aye, your Excellency,' whimpered the WI. And above their well-permed heads the lash cracked again, leaving a faint whiff of brimstone on the air.

Well of course this could not be allowed to go on. Using the cheese I had absent-mindedly carried from the lunch table I lured the Duchess into the potting shed and locked her in. Then I told the WI to keep what potatoes they had collected as a complimentary memento of a the garden visit of a lifetime, shooed them onto their coach and returned to the potting shed, where I threatened the Duchess with the police. She said sorry, something inside her had snapped, and calmed down a bit. She then cancelled all remaining bookings and spent a happy few days counting the season's gate money.

But you can only count money so many times. She went out under the pretence of sticking some hardwood cuttings into the propagating bed, and returned with the smug air of one who has just buried a taped-up biscuit tin of tenners somewhere clever. Then she sat down. Her eyes wandered around the room, and settled on the drinks cupboard. I thought oh, no . . .

The telephone rang. The voice on the other end was cultivated. It said it wanted to speak to the Duchess. I gave her the receiver, walked away and became preoccupied by a bullfinch which was strolling methodically along the branches of the wintersweet. It had the look of a bird that was in the middle of an excellent dinner, and expected several more courses after it had dealt with this one.

All the world knows that wintersweet is slow to flower, but I was beginning to realise why this particular specimen had held out on us for fifteen years. Another bullfinch touched down and joined the party. I turned to tell the Duchess about this, but she silenced me with an imperious hand.

'All right,' she said into the telephone. 'I'll send an article. You send a cheque.' She slammed down the phone, strode to her desk, and started hammering away at the old Underwood. After five minutes she stopped. 'That was the editor of *Gardens Unlimited*,' she said. 'He wants me to write about winter at the Hope. What on earth is there to say?'

'It is difficult,' I said. 'There is of course the usual stuff. But come to think of it, nowadays Helena Attlee is running a practical course on garden writing, called Open Ground (email: contactopen ground@gmail.com). They have already been to Sissinghurst, and it was a wild success. Why don't you try to get a place on that?'

She grunted. 'What beats me is how people in these garden magazines carry on writing the same old stuff, round and round. I mean spring, daffs, summer, lawns, and then autumn, leaves, and winter, well, what, eh? There is nothing to write about in the winter.'

I said, 'I'm sure Helena will sort you out.'

She shook her head. 'Perhaps I'll try.' She chewed the end off a Biro and spat the bits into a vase of hellebores. 'Garden writing,' she said. 'Round and round. I suppose it's money for old rope, really.'

'I wouldn't put it as strongly as that,' I said.

Health and Safety

A LITTLE WHILE AGO there was not even a rumour of spring. The kitchen garden slept under its Mypex. The rest of the place lay hard as iron, except for the wintersweet, which had decided to flower for the first time in its long, long life. The bullfinches did their best with the buds, but in the end the buds beat them, and they went zigzagging off into the undergrowth like disabled Dorniers, and a great peace descended.

But not for long. One morning the sky went black and the heavens made a prolonged and frankly alarming thundering noise. This shook the Hope to its foundations, or what would have been its foundations if it had any, though actually the house dates from a time well before such luxuries were even contemplated; and produced a musical jingle from the cupboard in which the Duchess's standing temptations are stored against the day of her relapse. Then it began to rain.

It rained and rained. Then it rained a bit more, and the neighbouring agriculturalists, whose minds are normally beginning to turn to potatoes at this time of year, took to nipping into the barn where we keep the boats and taking notes on ballast ratios and jib sheet leads. Just as they were talking about converting a silo into a sort of an ark type thing and leading the broiler chickens in two million by two million, the rain stopped, and the sun came out and shone with painful brightness upon the pleasaunces and messuages . . .

Yes. Painful is the word I used, and I used it advisedly. There is an ancient maxim that when women above thirty are being photographed, they should dive into the paintbox and slather on everything they can find, for the camera is a thing without mercy. The same goes for the sun and gardens in the pre-spring swampy period. The blue of the sky was intensely beautiful, and so were the yews, and the *Viburnum bodnantense*, glowing cherry-pink in the low sun. But that same sun glared down pitilessly on some terrible wrecks and eyesores in the borders. So while the Duchess sulked in the library, I went on a mission of purgation, using the tractor.

I may have described mechanised shrub removal before, but hey, a double dose of the right medicine is twice as effective as a single. It goes like this. Take a tractor and a very long rope. Attach one end of the rope to the shrub to be hauled out of the border. Carrying the free end of the rope, find a fair lead through the surrounding vegetation and attach it to the tractor. Then drive away.

On a normal day, the unfortunate shrub will shoot out of the ground like a missile from a silo, and you can then drag it to the bonfire. Not this time. The vegetable was a large and horrible ribes, with a root system resembling the Giant Octopus of the Pacific. The ground on which the tractor stood was about 5 per cent soil and 95 per cent water, and had gone thixotropic, which is what Heinz make sure happens to tomato ketchup, in that it looks solid, but is in fact liquid. The back wheels of the tractor began to turn. Tension came on the plant. The wheels began to spin. As they spun, they sank. I bailed out at the last minute, stopped the engine, and wondered what to do next. At this moment I became aware that I was being watched. By the Duchess, naturally. She had one eyebrow up, and was plainly in the grip of *schadenfreude*, one of the few emotions she actually enjoys, though it is doubtful she could put a name to it if you paid her. 'What now?' she said.

'Please do not interrupt,' I said. 'I am in the middle of an important experiment.'

'Is that what they are calling it this year?' she said. 'Looks pretty stuck to me. Why don't you plant some polyanthi in it?' Then she went off in a northerly direction.

At times like this, fuming is the only option, so I fumed. I kicked the tractor a bit, and revved it a bit, without result. Then I heard the noise of singing, and looked up. And what should I see advancing across the lawn with a wheelbarrowload of tools but the Duchess. Hi ho, she sang, hi ho. I asked her what on earth she thought she was doing.

'Getting you out of a jam,' she said. 'As usual.'

The injustice of this was so fierce that I began to prepare a riposte. But the Duchess had a spade, and was digging with a steady energy that made her look like a mole, if you can imagine a mole with bright red lipstick and rather marvellous diamonds. As she dug, she talked. 'When I was a gel,' she said, 'we all had our own gardens. And indeed gardeners. My personal one was called McTavish. He was a lazy beggar, so one had to knuckle down. It was where I learned my gardening.' I opened my mouth to observe that in my experience, her gardening consisted largely of drinking gin in the summer-house, and having to be retrieved from the cold frames claiming she was a little cutting that was putting out rooti-toot toots. 'The main part of it was digging. My main crop potatoes were the toast of the House of Lords, and Daddy adored my swedes. Unh. There.' She stepped back, dusting her hands.

The morass in which the tractor had been sitting had transformed itself into two long trenches, beginning at the back wheels and becoming gradually shallower as they rose to lawn level. I climbed on to the tractor, engaged reverse, and backed up the ramps and on to the lawn. The Duchess was squinting narrowly down the huge and hideous scars her excavations had left. 'What?' I said, over the chug of the engine.

'I always say,' she said, 'that a garden is scarcely a garden without an ornamental canal. Think of poor dear Louis.'

A great weight settled on my shoulders. In the Duchess's book poor dear Louis is Louis XIV of France, who is some sort of cousin of hers. She is a great admirer, though she has often said that his only fault was to have stinted on the building of Versailles, leaving it on the pokey side, and that that ghastly Le Nôtre was hardly fit to run a corporation allotment. 'A canal,' I said. 'What else?'

'Just a canal,' she said. 'You will be wanting to run along and order some concrete and plumbing materials, and to put in a call to that nice Mr Airsearescu late of the Romanian Securitate to round up some indentured labour. I am going to have a long long bath and a sit-down in the library. *The Cruel Sea* is on the telly.'

'Yes,' I said, but my heart was not in the word, for I had been watching her closely. Her tongue had nipped out, and run round her lips. The Duchess had had a triumph, and was in the mood to celebrate. Before you could say knife she would have jemmied open the corner cupboard, there would be empty gin bottles everywhere, and the air would be hazed with the choking blue fumes of Capstan Full Strength. 'Alas,' I said. 'There has been a localised incident. The library is out of bounds pending decontamination. You will have to watch the telly in the morning room.'

She protruded the bottom lip like a church doorstep. 'S'pose,' she said.

I shrugged. 'More than my job's worth. Not my decision, I am afraid. Out of my hands. Health,' I said, 'and safety.' Then I hurried off to underpin my argument by setting fire to the less desirable of the two sofas in the library. Goodness she was cross.

But a fortnight later, as I put the final touches to the Canal and I glimpse her looking out of her window in the tower, I can see that her sharp white face is almost benign. The daffodils are up, a pleasing sheet of pheasant's eyes against the reddish trunks of the Scots pines in the new Caledonian Glade. The scillas are the blue of angels' eyes and the carpet of crocus stretches deep under the eaves of the woods. The bullfinches no longer care about the wintersweet, because there are apples and plums to think about. Sated with buds, they are waddling around on their branches like bankers staggering home from lunch.

The world is on the turn again, and brightness is falling, and a flood of green is washing across creation. God, in short, is in his heaven, and so on and so forth. For the time being, anyway.